JEAN CRAIGHEAD GEORGE

ILLUSTRATED BY WENDELL MINOR

JULIE

This edition is published by special arrangement with
HarperCollins*ChildrensBooks,* a division of HarperCollins
Publishers, Inc.

Grateful acknowledgment is made to HarperCollins*ChildrensBooks,*
a division of HarperCollins Publishers, Inc. for permission to
reprint *Julie* by Jean Craighead George, illustrated by Wendell
Minor. Text copyright © 1994 by Jean Craighead George;
illustrations copyright © 1994 by Wendell Minor; cover
© 1996 by HarperCollins Publishers.

Printed in China

ISBN 10 0-15-365178-4
ISBN 13 978-0-15-365178-6

2 3 4 5 6 7 8 9 10   0940 17 16 14 13 12 11 10 09

To Cyd,
who loves the wind and snow
of the Arctic

CONTENTS

PART I

KAPUGEN, THE HUNTER   I

PART II

AMY, THE WOLF PUP 95

PART III

MIYAX, THE YOUNG WOMAN 161

PART 1

KAPUGEN,
THE HUNTER

A wolf howled. He began on a note lower than a bear's growl, then climbed the scale to the highest pitch of the wind and held it there.

The cry traveled across the snowy tundra and was heard by a young girl standing at the door of a small green house. The wooden structure sat on the edge of an Eskimo village on the bank of the frozen Avalik River in Alaska. She pushed back the halo of fur that framed her lovely face and listened. The wolf was telling her to come with him. She did not answer.

Julie Edwards Miyax Kapugen knew the wolf well. He had shared food with her when she had been lost on the endless tundra. He had run and played with her. He had rested in her tent while she had nursed him back to health from his bullet wounds. Now he was trying to locate her. He must not find her. He must go away, far away. After many years of separation, Julie was going home to her father,

Kapugen, and he, she knew, would kill the wolf.

"That is how it is," she whispered to the howler. "If you come near Kapugen, he will shoot you. He is like all Eskimo hunters. He will say, 'The wolf gave himself to me.'"

The howl rose and fell.

Julie squinted toward the distant caller. "Stay away, beloved Kapu. I am going home."

She waited. The wolf she had named Kapu after her father, the great hunter and leader, did not call again. Quickly she opened and closed the first door that led into Kapugen's house. She walked into the qanitchaq, an entry room designed to keep out the cold. Its walls were hung with parkas and boots, and on the floor stood paddles, guns, and gasoline cans. She put down her pack, took off her sealskin parka and maklaks, or boots, and hung them on pegs. She stepped to the second door, which opened into the living room, and hesitated.

She thought of her childhood on the Eskimo island of Nunivak in the Bering Sea, and of her maidenhood in Barrow on the Arctic Ocean. Then she thought of the day she had left that town desperate to end an arranged marriage. She had gone out on the tundra planning to walk to Point Hope and take a boat to San Francisco to meet her pen pal, Amy.

On the tundra wilderness she had become hopelessly lost.

She tried not to think about the lovable wolf pack that had felled a caribou and saved her life. She must put them in the past. She had found her beloved father and was going home to him.

Yesterday he had welcomed her in this very house. Her heart had lightened and her burden of loneliness had fallen away. Her head had danced with joyful thoughts.

Her happiness had not lasted long. Within a short time she had realized Kapugen was not the same father who had taken her hunting and fishing with the seasons on Nunivak.

He was not the father who had lived in grace with the sea and land. Kapugen had changed. He had a white-American wife, a gussak. He had radios, a telephone, and a modern stove. Julie could have accepted these things had not her eyes fallen on Kapugen's airplane pilot helmet and goggles. She had seen them on the man in the airplane window who had shot Amaroq, the magnificent leader of her wolf pack. This she could not reconcile. When Kapugen had left the house, she had put on her pack and returned to her camp along the barren river.

There, alone in the crackling Arctic night with

the hoarfrost spangling her tent with ice ferns, she knew she must return. No matter what he had done, Kapugen was her father, and she loved him.

"We do not judge our people," she heard the Eskimo elders say, and Julie pointed her boots toward Kapugen.

Now, only a wooden door stood between them.

She opened it and stepped inside. Kapugen was home. He was seated on a caribou skin on the floor sharpening his man's knife. He was alone.

He did not look up, although Julie knew he had heard her enter. She tiptoed to the iglek, a pile of furs stacked into a couch almost as tall as she. She climbed up on it, sat, and folded her hands in her lap.

Kapugen sighted along his knife to see if it was satisfactorily sharp. Julie picked a thread from her woolen sock. Kapugen selected a section of bearded-seal hide and cut a slender thong from it. He tied the thong around his boot. Julie sat quietly.

Presently Kapugen looked out the window at the marine-blue sky of the sunless winter day.

"The wind has died down," he said. "That is good."

"The stars are bright," Julie added.

"That is good," said Kapugen.

A silence followed. Kapugen tightened the boot

thong and at last looked at her.

"Did you hear the wolf?" he asked, looking into her eyes.

"I heard the wolf," she answered.

Another silence ensued. Kapugen did not take his eyes from her eyes. Julie knew he was speaking to her in the manner of the Eskimo hunter who communicates without sound. His eyes were saying that a wolf did not give that call of friendship very often.

Julie did not answer. She studied her father.

Kapugen was a stocky man with a broad back and powerful arms. His face was burned brown from the Arctic wind and sun, and his hands were blackened by frostbite. His hair was shorter than she remembered, but his chin was still smooth and plucked hairless. A faint mustache darkened his upper lip. He sat with his legs straight out before him.

"The wolf knows you." He spoke slowly and thoughtfully.

"He does," Julie answered.

Kapugen picked up the seal hide and cut another thong. Julie waited for him to speak again. He did not. He gave his knife one last hone and put it in the sheath on his belt. In one movement he rose to his feet and opened his arms. She jumped down from the iglek and ran to him.

After a long, comforting embrace, Kapugen lifted Julie's chin and touched the smooth olive skin of her cheek.

"I'm glad you came back," he said. "I was afraid I had lost you for a second time. I love you with the fullness of the white moon."

"That's a lot," she said shyly. He crossed his feet and lowered himself to the caribou skin, then patted it and invited Julie to sit. Julie saw the question on his face. She answered it.

"I broke the marriage arrangement with the son of your serious partner." Her voice was very soft.

"If a man and a woman," Kapugen said in a low, even voice, "do not love, they part company. That is the right way."

They sat quietly.

Kapugen, Julie saw, wanted to know more about her past, but, respecting her privacy, he did not ask. She must tell him no matter how painful her memories were.

"Do you not know," she asked in her gentle voice, "where I've been since that day Aunt Martha took me away from you to attend school?"

"I only know you went to Barrow when you were thirteen and old enough to marry," he answered, pacing his words slowly. "I happened to meet Nusan, your mother-in-law, in that town. She said you had run off and died."

"That was a terribly sad thing for her to say when she didn't really know," Julie said. "I am sorry. I will try to tell you what happened—perhaps not all— some things are still too sad."

Julie told him about her unhappy life in Mekoryok, the town on Nunivak, her days in Barrow, her marriage, and how deeply she feared Daniel, her angry husband. She recounted her days on the tundra with the gentle wolf pack and its kind leader, Amaroq, but she could not bring herself to say that Kapugen had killed him. The words would not form.

When she was done, Kapugen lowered his eyes for a moment, then looked up at her. His eyes said how much he loved her and how grateful he was that she was alive.

Julie buried her head on his shoulder, and he hugged her against his strong chest. This time as he held her, she felt forgiveness run up her spine and into her heart and mind. Kapugen, after all, was a provider for his family and village. Eskimo providers hunted.

"I am very tired," she finally said, her shoulders slumping. Kapugen brushed a strand of hair from her forehead. He lifted her in his arms, carried her to the iglek, and placed her upon it. She sank down into the sweet, soft furs and pulled a grizzly-bear skin over herself.

"I am glad you came home, Miyax," he said, and kissed her. She smiled to hear him call her by her Eskimo name. Like most Eskimos, Julie had two names, English and Eskimo—Julie Edwards and Miyax Kapugen. Hearing her father call her Miyax made her feel closer to him, and she decided she would let only him call her that. The name bound the two of them to her mother, who had given it to her, and to each other. To the rest of the people she would be Julie.

She closed her eyes and slept deeply.

"Good morning, Kapugen. Good morning."

Julie sat straight up in her furry bed and looked around. The man's voice was loud and crackly, but there was no one in the room. Kapugen came out of the bedroom.

"Good morning." He spoke to the glittering CB radio on the bookshelf. "Good morning, Atik. Good morning." Julie recognized the name of the hunter she had met with his wife, Uma, and baby on the frozen Avalik River. Astounded to hear him in the room, she slid off the iglek and sat on Kapugen's caribou skin, watching the radio and listening intently.

"Good morning, Malek," said a woman's voice. "Good morning."

"Good morning, Marie. Good morning."

For almost an hour the villagers of Kangik awoke and greeted each other on their CBs. Their voices filled the darkness of the sunless morning with cheer.

Ellen, Kapugen's wife, came out of the bedroom and, seeing that Julie was awake, greeted her.

"Good morning, Miyax," she said.

"Julie," she said softly but firmly.

"As you wish," said Ellen, and turned her back to dip up tea water from a thirty-gallon plastic container. There was no running water in frozen Kangik.

Julie studied Ellen. Her bright-red hair with its strange curls was an oddity to her, as were her pale eyes and eyelashes. Julie found herself staring and wondering about her father's new wife. When breakfast was over, she climbed up on the iglek and watched Ellen at her desk. She wrote in a book, glancing up at Julie now and then as if to ask if she was all right. Julie said nothing.

Next Ellen read a book. When lunchtime came around she even cooked by looking at a book. In the early afternoon Ellen phoned her mother in Minnesota.

"Hello, Mom," she said. "I have a daughter." She

smiled and glanced at Julie.

"Yes, she's pretty," Ellen said. "Beautiful smooth skin and big almond eyes. Her hair is as black and shiny as polished ebony." Embarrassed, Julie slid back under the grizzly fur and peered at her father's wife over the ruff. She wondered how this woman had gotten so far from home and why she did not go back.

"Want to say hello to my mom, Julie?" Ellen asked.

She did not answer. Julie knew English perfectly. Briefly she had forgotten it after Amaroq had been killed, but now she understood every word being said. She just did not feel like talking to Ellen.

Julie had been terribly disappointed to discover her father had taken a wife from the outside. To the Eskimos there are two peoples—the people within the circle of ice and the people outside it. Ellen was not from within. She moved and talked too swiftly. Her voice was harsh, and she laughed loudly like the jaeger seabirds.

Julie slowly adapted to her new life. She washed dishes and cooked fish and caribou meat for Ellen. She scraped skins and prepared them for the market, and she chopped ice in the river and put it in the container to melt.

She read Ellen's books when Ellen was out. Her English schooling in Nunivak had been excellent. She read the books avidly, eager to learn about the outside world. From time to time when no one was around, she would walk along the river and listen for her wolves. Once she heard Kapu, and looking around to see if Kapugen was outside, she cupped her hands and howl-barked a warning. Kapu replied with silence. He had gotten the message.

One day while Julie was scraping a bearded-seal skin to make boots, a new voice came in over the CB.

"Good morning, Kapugen. Good morning."

"Good morning, Peter Sugluk," said Kapugen. "You are back, are you?"

"I am back, all right," he said. "And I am picking up two qivit sweaters Marie asked me to bring to you." Julie recalled Uma telling her that the women of Kangik knitted sweaters and scarves from the warm, featherweight underfur of the musk ox. Kapugen, she had said, sold these incredibly warm clothes to merchants in Anchorage and Fairbanks for enormous prices, many hundreds of dollars.

"Come on over," said Kapugen, and turned to Julie. "Peter Sugluk is my business partner's adopted son," he said.

"He speaks with a strange accent," said Julie.

"It should not be strange," said Kapugen. "He speaks Yupik like we do, not Iñupiat like the people of Barrow and Point Hope."

The Eskimo language has two branches. Yuk, or Yupik, is spoken in southwestern Alaska and Siberia. Inuk, or Iñupiat, is spoken across northern Alaska, Canada, and Greenland. Julie had learned Yupik in Nunivak and Iñupiat in Barrow. Although she understood Peter, who spoke Yupik, she could not place his accent. She wondered where he came from.

Presently there was a rap on the inner qanitchaq door.

"Come in," called Kapugen, and Peter Sugluk stepped into the warm room.

"Good morning, Kapugen," he said, and glanced at Julie. "You must be Julie. Good morning." His smile was beguiling and friendly.

Julie looked up at a bronze-faced young Eskimo. He was tall. His nose was straight, his cheekbones high, and his eyes were bright half-moons under dark brows. He wore a tunic of reindeer over close-fitting leather trousers. His maklaks were of polar bear, trimmed with sled dogs in black-and-white calfskin. Ermine tails with black tips danced along the trim of his sleeves and boots when he moved. He looked old to Julie, perhaps eighteen or nineteen as compared to her fourteen, going on fifteen, years. She looked down at her sealskin and went back to her scraping.

"What they say is right," she heard Peter say. "You are beautiful."

Julie went on working. She did not want to be known for her beauty, but for her wisdom and fortitude, Eskimo virtues. She did not look up until he opened the door and was gone, but she thought she had seen him tap a toe and raise his palms in the dance symbol of celebration.

Two weeks passed. The days became turquoise blue as the earth tilted into the sun. By the time the bloody red ball came over the horizon on January twenty-second, Julie felt comfortable in her new home and village.

One day when Ellen was teaching at the school and Kapugen was at the desk poring over papers, she put down her work and stood before him.

"Aapa," she said softly, "I have been gone a long time on the tundra and I have been deep in a dream world with the wolves. Now I am awake. What can I do to help you?"

"That is good, all right," he said, looking up at her. Noticing that she was studying the papers he was working on, he spoke.

"These papers are the records of our musk oxen. Malek, Peter, and I keep track of them for the bank in Fairbanks. The bank finances our industry."

"Industry?"

"All Eskimo villages are corporations now," Kapugen said rising to his feet. "Unlike the American Indians, who live on reservations under government supervision, we run ourselves like a business. Our people own stock in the village corporation and share the profits." This did not make sense to Julie, but Kapugen seemed to think it was important, so she listened. "The Kangik Iñupiat Corporation is pretty big, all right," he said, pointing to numerals in the book. "We have a musk-ox business, a construction company, a store, and an electrical-generator company. We also get money from the oil taken from our land." She still did not comment, so Kapugen stood up and took her hands.

"Miyax, you must learn to hunt."

"I can hunt," she answered. "I can trap ptarmigan and snowshoe hares."

"You must learn to shoot a gun," he said. "We need you. Kangik is almost a deserted village. Many of the houses are empty, all right. The caribou have not circled back to us for two years, and the people are hungry. Many have moved to Wainwright and Barrow."

"That is too bad," Julie said.

"We are suffering," he said. "That is how it is." Kapugen went into his bedroom. He returned with a .22 rifle and cracked open the barrel.

"Is there really so much hardship in Kangik?" Julie asked. "I met your friends Uma and Atik up the river. Uma said that the people of Kangik make lots of money knitting musk-ox qivit into mittens and sweaters. She said you are raising musk oxen to help your village; and that you are a great leader."

"Uma is cheerful," Kapugen said, and smiled. "She was raised to admire a leader no matter what he does."

"I understand that," Julie said softly.

"You do, all right," he said, and looked at his helmet and goggles. "You do, all right," he repeated. Kapugen's face told Julie that her father now knew that the wolf he had shot from his plane was her friend. He looked very unhappy.

"Food is scarce in Kangik," he said, hastily changing the subject.

"Can't you fly your airplane and get gussak food for the village?"

"When the caribou fail to return, no white man's food can keep us healthy."

"The fish?" she asked.

"We also need flesh and fat to survive in the

cold," he answered. "And nothing tastes so good as the caribou and the whale."

Julie smiled. "That is true."

Kapugen slipped several bullets into the .22 and put on the safety so the gun could not be fired. He handed it to her. They went into the qanitchaq and put on their warmest clothing. Kapugen picked up his bear rifle. He put the carrying strap around his neck and rested the gun on his back. When Julie was dressed, he opened the door. The cold air sucked the breath from their mouths and swirled snow in their faces.

The sun was just rising, although it was ten o'clock. The rosy light illuminated a dip in the landscape that was the frozen Avalik River, and beyond it the huge platter that was Kuk Inlet. But for the village, a cluster of little wooden houses on pilings that kept them from melting the permafrost, all else was barren tundra.

Julie glanced at Kangik and held her breath. The village, which had seemed so vibrant on that first night she had laid eyes on it, was plain and dreary. Several of the houses were packing boxes in which snowplows and trucks had been shipped to the villages along the Arctic coast. Many were boarded up and deserted.

A dull murmur caught her attention.

"What is that?" Julie asked. "I hear it often at night."

"The electric generator," Kapugen said. "It runs on gasoline and makes electricity for our radios and stoves and lights."

The humming generator, sounding like a sleeping bear, gave a strange kind of life to the still, cold village. Julie listened for another sound. A dog barked once, a door squealed as it swung on its hinges, and a voice called out. The sounds were swallowed by the subzero cold. She listened more intently. There was no sound from Kapu.

Kapugen signaled her to follow him, and they walked east on the river ice in the somber polar light. After a short distance they both stopped and watched the sun light up the treeless, blue-green snow.

"You will like Ellen, I think, all right," Kapugen said after a while. Julie did not answer.

They went on up the river. Their footfalls smashed the ice into snow. It squeaked like glass, swirled up, and fell softly, making a trail of powder behind them. The sun had rolled along the horizon for almost an hour, and now it was setting. Kapugen turned to Julie.

"We will hunt foxes," he said. "Some live near the

musk-ox corral. Watch what I do. I learned to hunt in my father's boot steps. It is the best way."

Julie stepped in his boot tracks and followed him off the river ice onto the tundra. The ice fog that had arrived with the dawn began to thicken.

After a short hike Kapugen opened a gate, and he and Julie entered a large corral. Dark boulderlike forms loomed in the blue fog. Eleven musk oxen stared at them. Small clouds of frozen breath hung above their heads.

A wolf howled. Julie looked at Kapugen in alarm.

"The hunt is over," he said. "The foxes hide when the wolf howls."

"Ee-lie, Kapu," Julie whispered to the wolf, "stay away, stay far, far away."

Kapugen and Julie walked home.

Ice fog erased the landscape, and it was many days before Julie and Kapugen returned to the corral to hunt foxes again. They walked through a galaxy of sparkling ice crystals that floated over the quiet tundra. Kapugen led, and Julie stepped in his tracks.

After a long walk Kapugen stopped. He fixed his eyes on a distant spot, and Julie followed his gaze. A figure appeared and disappeared and reappeared like starlight on water.

"Lift your gun," Kapugen whispered. "When the fox stops moving, put the bead of the front sight into the notch in the rear sight. Click off the safety and pull the trigger slowly."

Julie fired and missed. Kapugen walked on, turning his head from right to left as he scanned the snowscape. His gun was slung across his back parallel to the ground; his hands were grasped behind him. He was alert to the most subtle movements and faintest sounds. Kapugen hunted like a wolf, and like a wolf he knew when there was no game. He stopped in the corral to check the uminmaks.

As he turned to go home, he kicked back the snow. It was not very deep, the wind having stripped the flat tundra of snow and exposed the grasses and sedges. For this reason the Arctic tundra was a perfect home for the grass-eating, well-garbed musk oxen. The tip of Kapugen's maklak touched an ancient ground birch that was only a seven inches high. He leaned down. Around it grew bilberry, Labrador tea plants, and a few dwarf willows.

"The uminmak's favorite foods," he said to Julie, then looked at the plants more carefully. "They have been eaten too close to the roots. The oxen are running out of wild food."

"The grasses are taller outside the fence," Julie

said. "Why don't you let them roam free?"

"So we can gather the qivit easily," Kapugen answered. "And," he added with bluntness, "so the wolves will not kill the oxen."

Julie felt a flush of blood run through her. She closed her eyes and swallowed hard.

"Soon," Kapugen said, "I must fly to Barrow to buy alfalfa pellets for the uminmaks. They need more food." He walked on. Julie placed her feet in his boot tracks.

"A white fox hide," Kapugen said turning to her, "brings fifty dollars in Fairbanks."

"Fifty dollars," Julie repeated to herself, and looked back toward the village. For the past seven months she had thought about no one but herself and her wolves. For seven long months she had directed all her thoughts inward toward staying alive. Now, as she walked behind her father, she knew it was time to become an Eskimo again, a person who helps the family and the village community.

She would not miss the next fox.

Julie not only followed Kapugen, she looked where he looked, she sniffed the winds he sniffed. When he stopped and listened, she stopped and listened.

A ptarmigan burst out of the snow and vanished

behind the ice cloud it had created.

"How much do they give for a ptarmigan?" she asked.

"Ten dollars," said Kapugen. She thought of the huge polar bear she had seen in Barrow. His great white hide must be so valuable, it could feed all of Kangik.

"How much do they give for nanuq?" she called above the wind.

"Nothing," replied Kapugen. "Only the Eskimos can harvest nanuq, the great white bear, and we cannot sell him. He gives himself to us. We give him to our people. That has always been so." Julie nodded.

They arrived at a three-sided shelter in the muskox corral. Snow was drifted high around the sturdy structure of heavy plywood. It was roofed with corrugated steel.

"This is where we put the hay and pellets for the uminmaks," Kapugen said. "It keeps the food from being buried under the drifts."

He looked up and smiled. Julie looked up too. A solitary bull was running toward them. She glanced at her father. Kapugen did not seem alarmed, and sure enough, when the bull was only a few yards away, he stopped. He ogled them. Shreds of qivit trailed from his shoulders.

The bull was massive but not very tall. He barely came up to Kapugen's chest. His huge neck muscles formed a hump on his back that was higher than his head. His tail was remarkably short, his hair so long it swept the ground like a skirt. His feet were enormous ice choppers. A bold boss of horn, curved tips pointed forward, met in the middle of his forehead like a helmet. The chunky rocklike animal bore a strong resemblance to the wooly mammoths of the past. He snorted.

"One of the last old-time animals," Kapugen said. "White men say he is a goat-antelope. To the Eskimo he is uminmak, the animal born to the ice and the wind and the snow." Kapugen held out a bilberry stalk to him. "Once," he went on, "there were millions of uminmaks in northern Alaska. When the Eskimo got guns, they shot them all. Every one.

"The U.S. government tried to bring them back. They got thirty-three calves from Greenland and set them free on Nunivak in 1930. When that herd was large, they brought some calves to Fairbanks and later set them free. We have a few wild ones on the North Slope now.

"The government helped me bring bull and cow calves to Kangik to start a qivit industry."

The bull snorted and pawed the ground, then

rubbed his head against his foreleg.

"Is he angry?" Julie asked.

"He is rubbing a gland near his eye on his leg. The scent from the gland warns the herd. It is not musk, as the white man calls it. It smells fresh and clean, like snow."

"What is he afraid of?" Julie asked.

"He is prey," Kapugen said. "He is concerned about all things; you, me, our guns, and the odors on the wind." Kapugen sniffed and squinted into the glaring snow. "He is saying the grizzly bear is awake."

"The grizzly bear?" Julie asked.

"Aklaq awakened last week in a warm spell," he said. "She has two yearling cubs and they are hungry. She has been staying close to the musk oxen, all right," he said. "That is not good. Like the wolf, the grizzly can kill an uminmak. Uminmak is smaller than a bear and not very bright."

Kapugen cupped his hands behind his ears.

"The herd is coming," he said, and smiled proudly. Out of a bright spot of ice glare the other musk oxen appeared, rolling along as if on wheels and seemingly pushed by the wind. They were a sturdy, well-knit group. The beasts slowed down, hesitated, then, circling like a whirlpool, forced the yearlings and calves into the center of their group for protection.

"They are alarmed," said Kapugen, looking around.

"The bear?" Julie asked, afraid that he was going to say wolf.

"I do not know," he answered.

The herd was quite close, and Julie could see the difference between the males and the females. The females were smaller, and their horns did not meet on their brows, as did those of the males. Both sexes had large eyes that protruded from their heads several inches. With these eyes they could see to the sides, the front, and the rear, and they could see in the dark as well as in the painful light of ice glare. The uminmaks are creatures honed by darkness, sun, and intense cold.

Kapugen moo-grunted.

A female left the group and came toward him. She hesitated when she saw Julie. Kapugen walked slowly up to her making soft sounds. When she was close, he reached out and scratched her head.

"This is Siku, Miyax," he said. "I found her on the tundra. Her mother had just been killed by a wolf pack. Siku was moving inside her. I opened the belly and lifted this little musk ox onto the ice—the siku; then I wrapped her in a caribou skin and took her home.

"I fed her on a bottle, and she lived and gave me the idea to raise musk oxen."

"Is it hard to raise them?" Julie asked.

"Not too hard," Kapugen replied. "Once, not too long ago, when the caribou were scarce, the people of Kangik, Wainwright, and Barrow raised reindeer. Malek was a herder. I met him and told him of my dream. He came to Kangik to join me. The state of Alaska gave us several more oxen to go with Siku. In time we had a herd and gathered qivit." Julie reached slowly out and touched Siku. The large eyes rolled her way, but the cow did not move.

"Siku," he said, laughing and rubbing her head roughly. "You started it all." She snorted and went back to the herd. The uminmaks had broken their fortress circle and were cropping grass.

"How many musk oxen do you have, Aapa?" Julie asked.

"Four bulls and seven females and yearlings. Not many, but the herd is growing. There will be four little calves in May or June if the wolves do not get them." He looked directly into her eyes.

Julie did not speak. She was thinking of that day on the tundra when an airplane came out of the mist and, with the burst of gunfire, killed Amaroq, the intelligent and kindly leader of her wolf pack.

She turned away from Kapugen's gaze. He was telling her he had killed the wolf to protect these musk oxen. He was thinking of his people, his eyes said, and they added that he would do it again if he had to.

Julie was terrified for Kapu and his pack. Wherever the caribou were, she fervently hoped her wolves were with them.

The sun, which had been up for two hours, was now sinking behind a horizon of ice mist. It glowed sparkling red, then disappeared. The long polar twilight entombed the top of the world as Julie and Kapugen turned homeward. In the short time it took to walk back to the village, the temperature dropped ten degrees. The wind gathered force. Kapugen pulled a bit of underfur from his parka ruff, wetted it, and held it up in the gale. It bent and froze in a hook.

"The wind is from the west," he said. "Tomorrow ought to be still and clear."

He pushed back his dark glasses and looked at the sky. "If the wind doesn't change in the night, tomorrow I will fly to Barrow."

"To get food for the uminmaks?"

"If I have time. Tomorrow I must take my wife to the doctor."

"Is Ellen sick?" she asked tentatively.

"She is pregnant," Kapugen answered, and smiled so broadly his teeth shone white even in the dark twilight.

Pregnant, Julie thought. A child would be born. She was both pleased and not pleased. The very thought of a baby stirred warm feelings within her, but she also knew she had found her father only to lose him again. She walked along in silence. Distant barks sounded in the purple dusk.

"The dogs," said Julie. "I often hear them bark. Are they yours?"

"I have a team," he said.

"But you have snowmobiles," Julie said. "You don't need a team."

"I have snowmobiles," he answered. "But I love the dogs."

"I love the dogs, too," she said, thinking of the wonderful animals who were descendants of the wolves.

North of the town they came to a large Quonset hut. It faced a flat windswept plain that was covered with a long sheet of steel chain.

"Airplane iglu," Kapugen said, pointing to the hangar. Here her father's airplane resided. "Airplane runway," he added, gesturing to the metal-mesh landing strip. "I must check out the plane for tomorrow. Do you want to see it?"

She really didn't. She did not want to see that airplane from which the fatal shots had come—ever. She still felt the pain of Amaroq's death. Inside that iglu were the wings of a father she did not know.

She took off her mitten and reached into her pocket. There she kept the totem of Amaroq she had carved to hold his spirit after his death. She clutched the totem and felt better.

"Coming in?" Kapugen asked.

"I'll keep hunting," she said. "A ptarmigan will bring ten dollars, and you can buy food for Siku."

"I have a treasure for you in there," he said, pointing to the Quonset with a broad smile. Julie drew back. She did not want to see that airplane.

"I have ermine," he said, reaching out for her hand. "Beautiful glistening white ermine. They are for you to make something regal for yourself." His eyes told of his love for her. "Come see them. They are in a box by the door. I was going to sell them to the furrier in Fairbanks, but when you came back to me, I wanted to wrap them around you. They are yours."

Kapugen opened a small door in the big door of the Quonset and held it for Julie.

"I must learn to hunt," she said, drawing away. "I will bring you a fox or a ptarmigan. Later I will come see my treasure." She smiled and backed around the corner of the Quonset. Kapugen went inside and closed the door.

A wolf howled.

Julie shut her eyes and wished that tomorrow would be clear and windless so the metal bird would take Kapugen and Ellen to Barrow. A day alone would give her an opportunity to call to her wolves and tell them to go far away from the hunter who would protect his oxen at all costs.

An hour before Kapugen was to depart for Barrow, the wind shifted.

Clouds darkened the skies over Kangik, and Kapugen changed his plans.

"Today we will stay home," he said, looking out the window as a gust of whirling, blowing snow whitened the town.

Julie's plans were also changed. She could not warn Kapu. She nestled down on the iglek and thought about her wolves. They would be curled in snow scoops, their noses in their tails, their feet tucked under them. Soon they would be as white as the storm itself. She smiled. They would not come after the musk oxen today.

Julie picked up the parka she was making to replace her old one and began to stitch a seam. She would line it with caribou fur, the best insulation known. When it was done, she could go out in temperatures of fifty degrees below zero and be almost as snug as her wolves.

Ellen, who had dressed for the trip to Barrow, changed back into her qaliguuraq, the long Eskimo dress that is flanked with a deep ruffle. Then she turned on the CB.

"Children of Kangik," she said in her harsh American voice. "There will be school today. Do you hear me, Roy, Ernie, Edna, Benjamin, Larry? There *will* be school today. Over." She opened the receiver switch.

"Morning, Teacher Ellen, morning," a child's voice said. "I hear you loud and clear. School today. Out." He sounded quite happy.

Ellen picked up her lesson bag and opened the door to the qanitchaq. As she passed the iglek, Julie noticed her figure for the first time. Her stomach was rounding out under her qaliguuraq. Julie wondered if the baby would have red hair.

At the door Ellen hesitated and turned to Kapugen.

"Kapugen," she said, looking at Julie, "would you ask Julie if she would like to come to the school with me today? She doesn't understand English. Please tell her I would enjoy her company."

"Miyax," he said softly, "minuaqtugvik?"

Julie shook her head to say no.

Ellen's pale eyes flashed. She asked Kapugen to insist. He smiled and tenderly kissed her cheek, but did not tell Julie to obey.

Ellen shrugged. When she opened the outer door, the wind rushed in, rattling the inner door; then Ellen was gone. Julie and Kapugen sat in silence. Kapugen picked up the book in which he recorded the items the villagers had given him to sell in Fairbanks. He opened it and then slowly closed it.

"Let's go fishing, Miyax," he said. "We can fish in the storm. We need more fish for the dogs and the villagers."

Julie slid down to the floor. "I would like that," she said.

"When we have many iqaluk," said Kapugen, "we'll store them in my game cellar." Julie nodded. The deep cellars in the icy permafrost kept fish and game frozen solid winter and summer.

"When we are done," he went on, "would you take the dog team out to duck camp for a good run? They need exercise."

"I would like to do that," said Julie, trying not to sound too eager. This was the opportunity to go out on the tundra and howl-bark to warn her wolves to stay away.

"I will fish with you until noon," Kapugen said as he worked. "Then I must come back. I am expecting a noon call from the chairman of the board of directors of the Kangik Iñupiat Corporation."

"How do I find duck camp?" Julie asked. She ignored the high-sounding title of the authority that could bring her father home from fishing.

"The dogs know the way," he said. "The black-and-white dog with the white eyebrows is CB, the lead dog. He will take you there and back with good spirit."

"That is good," Julie said, and put on her warm parka and boots.

In the quiet of falling snow Kapugen and Julie carried a fish net and ice choppers out onto the river ice. With his man's knife, Kapugen cut snow blocks and stacked them into a wall to break the wind. Then he reopened several holes in the thick ice—they had frozen over since their last use. He secured an end of the gill net above the ice, then dropped the net into one of the holes. He went to the next hole, reached into it with a long hooked pole, hooked the net, and brought it up. He secured a side of it with a stake and dropped the net again. Humming to himself, he went from hole to hole. In a short time he reached the last one and secured the end of the net to another stake. Then he went back along the line and pulled out all the stakes but the first and last. The net hung taut under the ice.

"My grandfather taught me how to drop a net." he said. "And his father taught him. Pass it along to your children, Miyax. It is a good method, all right."

"I will, Aapa," she said. "I will."

Kapugen spread his caribou skin and they sat down in the snow-block shelter to watch the clouds, the white river, and the land.

After a long wait Kapugen jiggled the net and felt fish. Together he and Julie pulled them out through the first hole, which was larger than the rest. About sixty silvery fish flopped on the ice. Kapugen took them from the net with his bare hands and put them in a twine bag. Julie dragged it to the ice cellar and dropped it in. Together they reset the net and sat on the caribou skin. With sticks they had brought from home, Kapugen made a small fire. The white walls reflected back the heat of the flame, and they were soon quite warm. Julie brought out some caribou jerky and a piece of frozen whale maktak. They ate quietly, watching the snow fall around them.

They chatted as they waited to bring more fish from the dark water beneath the ice. An aura of the father she remembered settled over Julie, and she felt completely content. Kapugen made them each a cup of tea, and the long years of separation seemed to have never been.

The snowfall became lighter and lighter until only tiny sparklets of ice floated in the air. Just before noon Kapugen returned to the house to wait for his phone call. Julie pulled up several more catches and then went out to harness the dogs.

She found Kapugen's six Alaskan malamutes behind the Quonset. They greeted her warmly, then burst into joyful barking when she took a harness off its peg on the back of the hangar. They knew they were going for a run. Each dog had its name on its harness and collar. She learned them before pulling the sled into the open and attaching the line. She stretched the line out on the snow, found CB's harness, and snapped him to it. Next she set the brake on the sled. Each dog she harnessed leaped, pranced, and pulled until she stopped talking to them in Yupik and spoke to them in wolf talk. She mouthed their muzzles to tell them she was in charge. They looked at her curiously and stood still. She had to yell at a dog named Minnesota, who she presumed was Ellen's dog. When that did not work, she growled at her and showed her teeth. Minnesota slunk away and stopped snapping at CB.

Julie hugged one of the gentle wheel dogs, Snowbird, then fastened his neck line to the lead. He whimpered his friendship. When they were all harnessed, but before she stepped on the runners at the back of the sled, CB lunged forward with such force, he pulled the brake out of the snow. The team was off.

Julie ran, grabbed the sled, and hopping aboard, threw all her weight on the brake, driving the long wooden prong deep into the snow. The team came to a stop. She walked up to CB, arms out to make herself look big and threatening. She put her mouth over his muzzle, then looked directly in his eyes.

"I'm boss," she said. CB lowered his tail and ears in submission, then licked her face. She laughed, rubbed his ears, and walked slowly to the rear of the sled, ready to growl if CB moved. As she passed by, the team members wagged their tails and whimpered to her.

"I love you, too," Julie said, happy to be speaking to these cousins of the wolves.

When she reached the end of the line, she slowly stepped up on the runners again. CB and his team waited respectfully for orders. Julie pulled the brake out of the snow but did not give a command to go. The dogs looked back at her to see what was the matter. She stood tall, her head high in the regal pose of Amaroq, who had led his pack with this silent language of authority. The dogs saw and wagged their tails. She grinned.

"Hut," she called, and the team took off.

She halted them at Kapugen's green boat to make sure she was in control. CB made a sudden lunge forward. Julie growled. He looked back at her, smiled with his mouth open, and wagged his tail once. He was saying he was sorry he had teased her.

Kapugen, who had been watching through the window, saw Julie and the dogs conversing. He grinned with pleasure. The spirit of the wild things lived in his daughter.

"Hut," Julie called, and CB and his team took off at a run. They soon left Kangik behind.

Through the snow sparklets Julie scanned the horizon for her wolves. She stopped at the corral gate to see if they had been there. The snow had covered the deep hoofprints of the oxen. The shallow tracks of wolves would be blanketed too.

"Hut!" she called, and the sled jerked forward. Minnesota pulled to the left and the sled tipped. Julie was about to be dumped when CB jerked to the right and the sled dropped back on both runners again. Bending his head to the task, he set a pace suitable for a long haul. As the sled slipped quietly out onto the flat tundra, Minnesota looked back at Julie with a wry eye.

"Ha," Julie shouted to her, "I'm still here. You did not knock me off." She laughed, Minnesota uncurled her tail to say she was disappointed, and CB led on, now listening attentively for Julie's commands. She did not have to give any. The sensitive dog followed the trail although it was buried under the snow.

Five miles on, CB pulled Julie and the sled into duck camp. He stopped before a cluster of little shacks that stood on a bend of the Avalik River. They were almost covered with drifted snow.

Julie untied the snowshoes on the sled, put them on, and tramped to one of the shacks looking for wolf sign.

"*Grrf!*" She froze. Aklaq, the grizzly, came around the corner and snorted a warning. Clumsy in her snowshoes, Julie ran the other way around the shed. The bear stopped and looked for her. Julie also stopped. She now had the shack between the bear and the sled. Reaching into her pocket for some of the uneaten maktak, she hurled it over the shack and dashed for the sled.

The bear stopped to gobble the whale blubber.

"Hut!" Julie called, clutching the sled ropes. The dogs needed no second order. They smelled grizzly bear. They ran. Julie threw herself on the sled, unstrapped her snowshoes, and climbed over the back board to stand on the runners. She and the dogs were a quarter of a mile away from the bear when she stopped them and looked back. No longer interested in Julie, Aklaq was digging in the snow for more maktak. Satisfied, Julie ran the dogs on.

"Halt," Julie called before the dogs had gone another quarter of a mile. They obeyed, but CB looked back at her as if to say she was out of her mind to stop when the smell of grizzly bear saturated the wind.

Julie had spotted two yearling bear cubs. They were digging near a den in the bank of the Avalik River. Kapugen was right: The mother grizzly was up early in the season, probably because her cubs were hungry. This was not good. The huge Aklaq could easily knock down the corral fence and take a musk ox.

Julie started the team again, calling "Haw" (left)

as soon as they were moving.

CB did not heed. He ran straight ahead. He did not want to go back toward the bears.

"Haw," Julie called with great force. CB finally pulled to the left. The two front dogs pulled right. The sled wove and tipped.

"Haw," Julie growled. The team went left, but too far. The sled tipped.

"Gee," Julie called, and dogs, traces, and sled straightened out and moved smoothly. By this time they were far from the big cubs, and CB held the course Julie had told him to take, northward over the tundra.

They were going along nicely when Minnesota snarled at her partner, Snowbird, then lunged at her neck. Julie howled a wolf command. They stopped fighting.

CB led his team over the snowy landscape for almost an hour while Julie scanned hummock and rise for wolves. Kapu and his pack were nowhere to be seen, nor were any foxes or wolverines. It was plain to Julie that the only wolf food in the vast area were the musk oxen.

A raven flew overhead. Julie stopped the team to watch this messenger of the tundra. The dogs lay down panting, even though it was ten below zero.

They bit snow to quench their thirst.

Ravens, Julie knew, were the first to find wolf kills and share the banquet with them. Eskimo hunters knew this and would follow the large black birds to find wolves. Julie guessed this flying bird could see fifteen miles in all directions. Since he was circling and flapping, he must not have sighted a wolf kill; he would be flying in a straight line to the food. The raven was fluttering and diving, which meant he was hunting lemmings. Julie was discouraged. For at least fifteen miles in all directions there were no wolves. She turned back.

A roar reached her ears as over a rise in the land a snowmobile appeared. She waved.

The driver pulled his vehicle up beside Julie's sled, but it was not until the man pushed back his dark snow glasses that she recognized Atik.

"The weather has turned nice," she said. "Are you hunting?"

"I am scouting for caribou," he said. "The females should be coming to Kangik now. They come ahead of the bulls. They will calve on the tundra in May."

"Did you find any?" she asked eagerly.

"There are no caribou from Kangik to Anaktuvuk, more than two hundred miles away," he said. "I have just talked to David Bradford, the Alaska Fish and Game man. He told me that. He brought his helicopter down near me. He said he heard the beeping of one of the radio collars he puts on moose to learn where they go."

"Where was the moose?" asked Julie with some excitement.

"There was no moose," he answered. "The collar had fallen off. He found it on the ground. Sometimes that happens, he said."

Julie scanned the frosty horizon.

"Do you think the caribou will come to Kangik this year?" she asked.

"They will not come. It is too bad," said Atik. "Kangik will suffer."

"When I first met you on the river," she said hopefully, "I told you of a small herd I had seen. Did you find them?"

"I never did," he said. Julie was surprised.

"I saw their tracks," Atik said. "They disappeared in the drainage passes."

"Did you see any wolves today?" she asked.

"David Bradford saw a pack from his helicopter," Atik said.

Julie's heart beat furiously. "Where were they?"

"Not far from here. He said the leader was a big black fellow."

"Kapu," Julie said under her breath. "Did he say how many wolves were in the pack?"

"He said eight."

"Eight?"

"He saw the black wolf and a white one and three dark-gray and three light-gray wolves."

The white one was Silver, she said to herself. The three light-gray wolves would be Zit, Zat, and Zing, the now-grown-up pups. The dark-gray wolves would be Nails and Sister, but who was the third dark-gray wolf, Julie wondered. Had Kapu taken a mate? It was, after all, time for pups.

Atik saw that the sky was magenta and turning blue-black. The sun was below the horizon. The long twilight was over and night was upon them. He nodded to Julie and sped off.

CB watched him go and then looked at Julie.

"All right, CB," she said. "Hut!" She sent them straight out on the tundra again. She smiled at the eager dogs, who kept looking back at her wondering why she was not going home.

"We're circling the bears," she called. Then after a short while she shouted, "Haw," and brought them back to the riverbank. CB joyfully broke into a run. The only sound as the moon came up was the swish of the runners and the panting of the dogs.

Julie threw back her head and reveled in the cold beauty of the night. She was worried, though. Her wolves were nearby and the only food for them was musk ox.

The wolves did not call during February, March, and early April. Julie relaxed. She took their silence to mean they were hunting caribou in the Brooks Mountain Range, about eighty miles south. But just as Atik had predicted, this also meant that no caribou would come through Kangik again this year. That was not good news. The families that needed four or five caribou each year to sustain their lives were leaving Kangik and moving in with relatives in bigger towns. Others were wandering in search of food as they had before white men came to Alaska. Atik went to the coast and brought back a walrus for his family. Malek made plans to go whaling on the sea ice.

One morning Peter came to Kapugen's house and Julie answered the door.

"Kapugen is in Fairbanks," she said.

"That is too bad, all right." Peter's dark brows stitched together. "Malek and I have been invited to join a whaling crew in Wainwright. I had hoped I could leave the musk oxen in Kapugen's care for several weeks. I see I cannot. He is gone and Malek is leaving today." He turned to go.

"I will take care of the uminmaks," she said. He spun around quickly.

"Would you?" His even teeth shone white against his bronze skin as he smiled broadly. "The villagers are hungry for maktak, Miyax," he said. "They need that good whale skin and blubber to lift their spirits. They all will thank you if we are lucky."

"Go along," she said. "I like to be out with the oxen on the tundra, and I know what to do. Kapugen has taught me."

"Ee-lie," he said, and lifted his arms in celebration. He ran off as swiftly and lightly as a tundra bird.

When he was gone, she wondered why she had not corrected him when he had called her Miyax.

That very afternoon she took over the musk-ox chores. It was a pleasant day. She hitched the dogs to a sled load of hay and alfalfa pellets and rode out to the shelter. She counted the herd, as Kapugen always did, and noted that the grasses were thrusting up through the rotting snow. Then, according to Kapugen's routine, she drove the dog team around the corral to make sure none of these hardy beasts with their muscular bodies had damaged the fence. Finally, work done, she turned the dog team east and ran them along the riverbank. The air was so cold, the frozen breath of the dogs left a long white vapor trail behind them.

At duck camp she stopped and listened for Kapu and his wolves. She heard nothing.

"They are gone," she said happily, then added, "Stay away, dear Kapu, stay away."

As she mushed home free from worry, she felt like a wolf running great distances for the pure joy of it. The wind blew back her wolverine ruff, and she leaned forward and sang her qimmiq, or dog, song.

> *"Wise qimmiqs, brave qimmiqs,*
> *Run with your tails up.*
> *Run with your tails up.*
> *When wind bites and cold numbs,*
> *Run with your tails up.*
> *Run, qimmiqs, run,*
> *In life's stormy weather,*
> *Run with your tails up.*
> *Ee-lie, ee-lie, ee-lie, ee-lie. La, la, la la."*

The dogs wagged their tails in rhythm to the song and now and then looked back at Julie and smiled.

———

Ellen closed the school in mid-April. The hunting season had begun. The parents who had not gone to the coast for whale and seal had taken their children inland to duck camp. The waterfowl were returning from the south in long black ribbons. Every half hour or so a band of thousands and thousands of eider ducks passed over Kangik, skimming low along the ground and over the houses as they migrated home. Julie would watch them, her head back, her eyes half closed, and she would wonder what magic brought them back each year.

On a sunny day in May, before the sun came up to stay for three months, Harry Ulugaq drove up to Kapugen's house on his three-wheeled motor bike. He brought a basket for Kapugen to sell in Fairbanks. It was made from fine strips Harry had cut from a piece of bowhead-whale baleen, the long, narrow filters in the whale's mouth.

"The museum would like this," Kapugen said after admiring the glow of the very black baleen and the symmetry of the work of art. "But I can probably get more from a collector—perhaps thirty-five hundred dollars." Harry nodded. He was one of the last baleen artists on the Arctic coast and knew well the value of his craft. But this day he had more exciting matters on his mind than money. After Kapugen listed the basket and its worth in his book, Harry went to the window and pointed toward Kuk Inlet.

"We have good luck," he said as Julie came up beside him. "A southerly storm has brought millions of smelt to the open water at the sea end of Kuk Inlet." His eyes twinkled. "Lots of fun."

"Lots of good eating," Kapugen said. "I have a fine market for smelt. Lots of Barrow families find it a treat."

When Kapugen had seen Harry Ulugaq to the door, he returned to Julie and Ellen.

"It's time for us all to go fishing," he said with a broad grin. "Smelt fishing is good fun, all right."

"Who will feed the musk oxen?" Julie asked.

"I fed them well today," said Kapugen. "We will not be long. The grasses are growing fast in the new sun, and they will find much to eat."

"Good," said Ellen, getting down the camping food box. "I'll pack enough food for a week. Kapugen, get the tent and sleeping skins."

Smelt camp was lively. Families slept in tents and mingled outdoors. Julie fell easily into the rhythm of community life. She and the older children helped lift the nets, clean and split the fish open, and put them on drying racks. Two or three days later, when the fish had dried in the sun and air, they helped pack them in boxes.

When the tide came in, Julie went to the shore to watch the glistening clouds of smelt swim in from the sea. When the tide turned, Julie and her friends would walk down the beach with the ebbing water to find the deep pools where thousands of fish were trapped. They would throw nets over them, and the men and women would hurry from camp to help pull the fish out of the water and up to the drying racks.

Between tides, the young people raced snow-mobiles out on the tundra or drove them back to the Kangik store for gasoline and staples. Sometimes Julie rode with them, but she preferred to paddle the umiaq along the edge of the ice that filled the upper inlet and watch the snowstorm of birds nesting and defending territory. Julie also watched the side streams to see if the graylings, Kapugen's favorite fish, were spawning in the shallows yet.

At fish camp no one looked at watches. The sun was up almost twenty-four hours each day. Children napped and ate when they felt like it. The adults slept when the tide was in and fished when it went out. Between work and sleep adults and children played one-foot-high kick—a game played by kick-ing a fur ball on a thong hung one foot above their heads. They rolled kayaks and chased each other like wolf pups. Harry Ulugaq organized a baseball game, and then everyone danced away the rosy hours before the sun set briefly.

When the winds changed, the smelt did not return to the Kuk Inlet. Tents came down, and barrels of the dried fish were loaded onto snowmobiles and taken home to game cellars or to the Quonset to be flown to Fairbanks and Barrow.

That evening a radio message came from the Eskimos in Anaktuvuk Pass. They reported that the caribou of the western herd were moving northward on the easternmost border of the great circle they took from south to north to south. They would not come through Kangik. Hearing the final word, many families went out to the coast to hunt seal and beluga whales.

On May tenth, the sun did not set. The North Pole had tilted full into the sun for the next three months. The white fox turned gray-brown and the ptarmigan became splotched with white and blue-gray feathers to match the snow-and-grass-mottled tundra. The pretty white-and-black snow buntings returned from the south and hopped through the village streets. Feeding them bread crumbs made a good excuse for Julie to run outside and up the river shore to listen for her wolves. They did not call.

One clear day in late May Kapugen arranged to take the airplane to Fairbanks to attend a meeting of the corporation officers and the bankers. He carefully wrapped Harry's baleen basket, a lovely sweater, and the pelts of the four white foxes that had given themselves to Julie. She had skinned and prepared them for the market after making the meat into stew for her family. She asked Kapugen to buy musk-ox pellets with the money they brought.

"That will help the industry," she said, still somewhat unsure of what she was talking about.

Julie was fishing when Kapugen, the furs and artifacts in a pack on his back, came down to the river shore to speak to her. The constant sun had softened the ice, and it was too dangerous to stand on and fish. The breakup was imminent.

"Miyax," he said, "my plans have changed. Harry Ulugaq is very ill. I am taking him to the hospital in Barrow." He walked a few steps closer. "I am worried about Siku. I checked her this morning. She is bawling and her calf is not due for many weeks, I think. I cannot stay to help her."

"I will go to Siku," Julie said, and followed him into the house. Ellen, who was enjoying music on her cassette player, turned down the volume to listen to Kapugen tell her that Julie was going out to the corral to check on Siku. Then he turned to Julie, gave her pills to relax his favorite ox, and showed her how to make Siku swallow them.

"And Miyax," he said as he crossed the room, "you had better walk. It is almost forty degrees, too hot to run the dogs."

He hurried out the door, and Julie and Ellen were alone. Ellen watched Julie pack the medicine; her ulu, the woman's knife; needle and thread; and a change of clothes.

"I would like to go with you, Julie," she said in barely understandable Yupik. "I need the exercise." Julie listened to Ellen labor over the words, and although Julie could have easily told her in English to come along with her, she did not. She still did not have it in her heart to speak English to Ellen. She nodded instead.

Ellen dressed warmly in many sweaters, her parka, down pants, and fur-lined sealskin boots. It was still May, but the weather often played tricks.

Julie opened the house refrigerator and stowed cheese and bread in her pack. Since she did not know how long Siku might be in trouble, she also packed a large quantity of dried caribou from the jerky barrel. Then she rolled up a caribou skin to sit on and tied it to the bottom of her pack. Finally she took down

Kapugen's man's knife from the wall and slid it under her belt. She hung her gun across her shoulder.

"Itqanait" (I am ready), she said and hurried out of the house.

They watched Kapugen's plane take off and head into the sun, and then, side by side, they walked the riverbank. The river ice had cracked like a jigsaw puzzle and was beginning to move. It heaved and creaked.

"The breakup is late this year," said Ellen in English. She had to talk even if she thought Julie did not understand. "Kapugen said it will be vicious when it goes."

As they walked, Julie pointed to a king eider duck on the ice. He was a gorgeous bird, with his orange-yellow-and-green head and black-and-white back. "Qinalik," Julie said. Ellen repeated the word three or four times. A white-fronted goose was feeding in the slushy water in the reeds. "Niglivik," said Julie, and Ellen repeated that.

When they arrived at the corral, Siku was standing near the shelter. Her fur was rumpled and her large eyes were glazed. Julie ran to her and gently rubbed her head and back while speaking softly to her. The ox wobbled and stumbled forward. Her big knees buckled.

"She's ill," Ellen said. "She mustn't die. We need her so."

Julie glanced at her. Ellen had spoken with great feeling.

Quickly Julie took off a boot thong and, tying it around Siku's neck, led Kapugen's favorite animal into the shelter. Ellen spread hay for her. Siku went down on her knees, then rolled to her side with a moan. Her huge cloven feet plopped heavily to earth.

Julie spread the caribou skin and indicated to Ellen that she should sit down. Then she took one of the extra woolen socks from her bag and rolled it in the snow. She placed it inside her parka. The snow quickly turned to water, and she dripped it between Siku's parched lips. The animal drank and lay still. Julie opened Siku's mouth, placed the pill on the large tongue, and held her mouth closed as Kapugen had instructed. Siku swallowed the pill. Julie gave her more water.

Ellen put her hand on the ox's large belly. "She's in labor," she said, surprising Julie with her expertise. Siku lifted her head, rolled her eyes, and lay still.

For an hour Julie and Ellen watched her strain to give birth until she could strain no more. The calf would not be born.

Julie thought of Oliver Ahgeak, who, like Malek,

had been a reindeer herder in his youth. He was still in the village. He would know what to do.

"Oliver Ahgeak," Julie said, pointing to Siku, then gesturing to say she would go get him.

Ellen nodded and Julie turned to leave. She drew back. A dark, sinister cloud was rolling down upon them.

"Hilla, the weather spirit," Julie said in Yupik. "It has turned against us. This is a storm to be dreaded." Knowing Ellen did not understand, she pointed to the cloud. Ellen, who had seen many bad storms in her three years in Kangik, looked at this one and drew in her breath.

"You can't leave now," she said. "What do we do?"

Julie was on the move. She drew Kapugen's knife from her belt and tramped to the lee side of the shelter, where the last snow of the season was packed high and hard. With consummate skill she cut blocks. They were about three feet long and two wide. They were almost six inches deep. Working quickly, she stacked them to make a wall on the open side of the shelter. Ellen, seeing what Julie was doing, took the blocks from her as she came around the end of the shelter and stacked them. Swiftly, Julie used more snow as a plaster to keep the wind from blowing through the cracks. The wall went up. When there were but two more bricks to lay, the wind struck with such force the wall buckled, but held. The gust brought snow so dense that Julie could not see the shelter although she was right beside it. Feeling her way with one hand, she rounded the corner with a last brick and crawled inside. She sealed the wall with the block.

They huddled in the gloomy shelter. Even the constant sun could not penetrate the blackness of the storm.

"How long will this last?" Ellen murmured to herself and listened to the shrill wind. Julie patted more snow against the inner wall, then took from her pack a small jar of the whale blubber she used to grease her ulu and gun. She made a wick for the jar by cutting a slender bit of cloth off the bottom of her shirt and lit it with a match from her pack. The tiny light flickered, almost went out, then drew oil and brightened. The shelter glowed and warmed. Ellen smiled gratefully.

The wind thundered against the north end of the shelter and Julie looked anxiously at Ellen. Her face was amazingly calm.

Siku bawled weakly.

"We've got to deliver this calf," Ellen said.

"How do we do it?" Julie asked in perfect English.

Ellen stared at her. "You speak English."

"Yes."

Ellen frowned perplexedly, but Julie told Ellen with her eyes that she had come to like her. Then she looked down at the cow.

Water flowed from the birth canal and Siku groaned. Ellen got down on her knees; Julie knelt beside her.

"The calf is coming out rear feet first," Ellen said. "That's the wrong way. It'll never make it, and neither will Siku."

The wind shook the shelter. Fine bits of ice sifted in through the snow bricks despite Julie's caulking. They settled like flour dust on everything.

"I'll cut her open, like Kapugen did to her mother, and take the calf," said Julie.

Siku tried once more to deliver the calf. Her tongue rolled from her mouth, swollen and dark purple, and she gave up and lay still. Julie picked up her ulu.

"In Minnesota," Ellen said, "we reach into the womb and turn the calf around." She tore off her parka, rolled up her sleeves, and plunged her hand deep into the womb. Julie was astounded. Siku lifted her head, then relaxed her abdomen.

"Hobble her feet so she won't kick," Ellen said. Julie removed her boot thong from Siku's neck and tied her rear feet down. When Siku thrashed, Julie lay across her neck and whispered soothingly into her ear.

Perspiration poured from Ellen's face as she slowly but correctly turned the calf. Its forefeet appeared, then its head.

"Help me to get Siku up on her feet," Ellen said. Julie slid off the uminmak's body and, reaching under her shoulders, lifted the laboring Siku to her feet. As she arose, the calf slipped from her body onto the hay. Siku wobbled and sank back, exhausted.

"A girl," Ellen said. "Good. Unclog her nostrils of mucus."

Julie cleaned the calf's nose; Ellen blew into her mouth. The calf sucked in air and breathed. She was fully formed and fat. Apparently Kapugen had the delivery date wrong. Julie reached into her pack for her extra shirt and wiped the calf dry. It got to its feet and wobbled to its mother's side. She arose slowly and the calf nursed. Julie and Ellen looked at the newborn and relaxed.

"It's gotten awfully cold," Ellen said. "I hope the little thing makes it."

"She will," said Julie. "She's a musk ox. She was made by a storm."

Ellen smiled. Shivering, she pulled out a red bandana, wiped her hand and arm clean, and put on another sweater and parka.

The wind gusted, blasting more fine snow through the cracks. Julie picked up the whale-blubber lamp and held the flame near the block seams. The heat melted the snow, which quickly turned to ice and ceiled the inside of the wall.

In a short while Siku delivered the afterbirth.

"She will eat it," Ellen said. "It gives her protein and vitamins."

"That will take too long," Julie said. "There is a grizzly who travels this area. She would knock down the fence and our shelter for such food."

"In a storm like this?"

"It is nothing to her. She has two yearling cubs to feed," Julie replied.

"What do we do?"

"I will take the afterbirth outside the corral," Julie said, and put on her parka.

She wrapped the afterbirth in hay, pulled out the bottom snow block, and crawled out into the storm. The wind stung her face with snow darts. A powerful gust knocked her to her knees. When she struggled back to her feet, she could see nothing but snow— no ground, no sky, no up, no down. She was inside Hilla, the all-white weather spirit. She could not even see her knees. She would have to crawl. Crawling would make a deep trough that she could follow back to the shelter. She put the bundle in her parka, touched the totem of Amaroq, and moved out into the storm. Finally, she found the gate and threw the afterbirth as far as she could.

Then she turned and dropped to her knees to crawl back. The trough she had dug was not there. In one instant the wind and falling snow had leveled it. Julie shivered even in her caribou-lined coat. She had absolutely no idea which way to go.

"Ellen," she called.

No answer.

"Ellen!" The wind stopped her words before they could leave her mouth. She turned her back on it and let the wind carry her voice on its speeding journey.

"ELLEN! ELLEN!" No reply. Ellen, she realized, could not hear her over the shrieking gale. Knowing better than to move, she waited until there was a lull in the wind screams.

"ELLEN! ELLEN!"

"Julie, where are you?" The voice was so faint, she could not tell from which direction it had come.

"Shout, Ellen, sing! I can't find my way back."

"Julie. Julie. JULIE," Ellen shouted over and over, and Julie, hanging on to the sound as if it were a rope, crept forward. Her head hit the snow wall. She pulled back the block and crawled in.

"You look like ugruk, the seal," Ellen gasped, brushing snow from Julie's parka.

"I guess we are not going anywhere tonight," Julie said. "And maybe not tomorrow night, either," she added.

The hours crept by. Julie and Ellen stomped their feet to keep themselves warm, ate dried caribou, and huddled against Siku's warm body. The roar of the wind grew ever louder.

"Hilla will not go away," Julie said.

"What do Eskimos do now?" Ellen asked. She patted the calf, who was curled beside her mother.

"We sing and we eat and we wait," Julie said. "We do not move."

"I am shivering," Ellen said.

"Siku's skirt is long and very warm. Wrap your hands in it and blow on them." Ellen tucked her hands and feet in the incredibly light and warm fur, and she stopped shivering.

They sat quietly in the cold gloom. Finally Ellen spoke.

"You speak beautiful English, Julie," she said. "I did not know that."

"I lost my English voice on the tundra," Julie said, "when Amaroq, a noble black wolf who had befriended me, was shot. He saved my life."

"He saved your life?"

Ellen looked as if she would like to hear the story, but Julie could not bring herself to speak about it. Someday she would tell Ellen about Amaroq, someday when she could tell the story without crying.

"Anyway," Julie went on, "the truth is my knowledge of English came back to me when I saw Kapugen's house, but . . ." She looked at Ellen.

"I understand," she said. "I am glad you've decided I'm okay."

"You are. You are," Julie said, her eyes shining.

In silence they warmed their hands and feet on Siku and listened to the wild raging storm. The whale-blubber lamp glowed. They did not close their eyes.

Long hours later Ellen sat up.

"Do you know the words to 'The Far Northland,' Julie?" she asked.

"No," Julie answered, laughing at the title. "Please teach me. This is the perfect place to learn a song with that name."

Ellen cleared her throat.

> "It's the far northland that's a-calling me away,
> As take I with my knapsack to the road."

Julie's eyes twinkled and she clapped her hands to her mouth. "What's next?"

> "It's the call on me of the forest in the north,
> As step I with the sunlight for my load."

"Go on."

> "By Lake Duncan and Clear Water
> And the Bear Skin I will go,
> Where you see the loon and hear its plaintive wail.
> If you're thinking in your inner heart
> There's swagger in my step,
> You've never been along the border trail."

"Teach me, teach me," Julie cried.

By the time Julie had learned the chorus and all the verses to the song, Ellen was nodding and she herself was very sleepy. She checked Ellen to make sure her face was not freezing, then curled up against Siku and dozed.

The storm roared on and on. Julie and Ellen did not know how long they had been in the shelter or what day it was. They would open their eyes, listen to the wind, melt snow for tea, take a bite of cheese and bread, and close their eyes again. Ellen did not complain. The warm Siku and Julie's insulated wall were keeping them from freezing to death.

When Julie saw that Ellen had awakened during a furious blow and could not go back to sleep, she ventured to ask why she had come to the North Slope. Ellen rolled up to a sitting position, hugged her knees, and stared at the cheerful whale-blubber light.

"Like the song says," she began, "it was the far northland that was 'a-calling me away.' When I got my master's degree in education from the University of Minnesota, I saw a newspaper ad for a teacher in an Alaskan village. I could think of nothing more inspiring than that. I applied to the North Slope Borough, was interviewed, and got the job. I was sent to Kangik." She looked up at Julie. "Believe it or not, I liked it."

"Was my father here then?"

"He was here. We met the day after I arrived and soon fell in love. It was that simple. I called home and told my mother I was marrying an Eskimo."

"What did she say?"

" 'Is he kind?' "

"What did you say?"

"'That's why I love him.'" Her face softened and then she smiled. "When I married Kapugen, I had no idea I would face so many hardships, even though I grew up on my grandfather's farm in Minnesota."

"Minnesota has trees," said Julie.

"And all that goes with trees: flowers, warm sunshine, hot and cold running water, flush toilets, bathtubs . . ." She looked into the yellow flame. "Yet I do not want to go back, and particularly now that I am going to have an Eskimo child."

"Yes," said Julie confidently. "He will be happier here. We like Eskimo babies of all shades, and especially with red hair."

Ellen laughed heartily. "Maybe he'll have black hair and red eyelashes." That made them laugh even more.

"Did Kapugen have the corporation when you met him?" she asked.

"Kapugen was just starting the musk-ox business when we married. The corporation paid for his training as a pilot. The only way to do business on the North Slope is by plane. We lived in Fairbanks during his training. He returned several times to Nunivak to find you. No one except Aunt Martha knew where you had gone. And she was dead. No one knew what had happened to you. Kapugen came home depressed and discouraged from each trip. He would talk endlessly about you and how you and he would hunt and fish together after your mother died."

Julie listened to this story about a man and a little girl he could not find. It seemed like a folktale about people she did not know.

"On a trip to Barrow last fall," Ellen went on, "Kapugen happened to meet Nusan, the wife of Naka. She told him that Naka was dead. Then she said with bitterness that you had just run from your marriage to her son, Daniel, and gone inland. She said you had died on the tundra."

"He told me that," said Julie. "But what then?"

"When Kapugen came back from Barrow, he kayaked up the Avalik for almost a week to grieve alone. Then he came home. 'That is how it is,' he said. 'It cannot be helped.' And we decided it was time to have a baby." Julie bowed her head, over-whelmed by the knowledge that she had been sought and talked about all this time.

"You must know the joy he felt when you knocked at his door," Ellen said.

"And to think I almost did not come back," Julie said softly. "When I realized he had killed Amaroq, I could not bear to be with him."

"I didn't know he killed your friend."

"It is still very hard for me to understand Kapugen," Julie said, her eyes glistening. "He did not even use the valuable fur."

"Wolves kill oxen," said Ellen.

"Is that his reason?" Julie asked softly.

"I think it must have been," she said. "He was worried about wolves at that time."

"But the other man? Who was he?"

"A gussak who had paid him well to take them both wolf hunting. White hunters hate wolves. They kill the caribou and deer they want."

Julie sighed and leaned against Siku. Ellen turned over on her side. The wind shook the shelter, and snow sifted down upon them. The little calf was resting and the mother was breathing quietly. They all fell asleep.

After a long time had passed, Julie was awakened by a change in the wind song. It had lost its rage. She pulled back a snow block and looked outside. She could see.

Ten snowy musk oxen stood in a circle around the shelter, their soft brown eyes upon her.

"Friends," she called, taking down another block and carrying pellets to them, "you have a new clan member."

As she crawled through the opening, she observed the sky.

"Ellen," she said, "there's no light to be seen where the sun should be. I think we are here for a few more days." Ellen did not say a word. Julie scrambled back into the shelter, took out the cheese and bread, and melted tea water in a tin cup over the whale-blubber candle.

"Can you teach me more songs, Ellen?" she asked. Ellen had many more to teach her. They sang the hours away.

Many hours later the interior of the shelter grew lighter and lighter. The wind stopped shrieking. Julie stuck her head outside.

"Ellen," she called exuberantly, "the sun is shining. We can go home."

Siku and her calf, whom Julie had named Far Northland, watched Ellen and Julie tear down the snow wall and let in the sunshine. As Julie and Ellen ran toward the gate, Siku and Far Northland followed them. The herd rubbed their eye glands against their forelegs, and the mother and calf smelled this message of warning. Siku nudged her calf and turned back toward the herd. Her long fur swung around her feet as she walked slowly into the sun sparkle. The oxen gathered around her and looked long and steadily at the new baby.

Singing happily, Julie and Ellen opened the gate and started out across the hard, wind-pounded snow. It squeaked under their footsteps and boomed as if they were walking on a drum. In a short distance they came upon strewn hay and the claw marks where Aklaq had found the afterbirth. They looked at each other knowingly and plowed down the river trail.

Three wolves howled, first one at a time, then in unison. Julie's heart beat wildly. "Go away, go away," she cried inside herself. "Go away."

Ellen was singing and seemed not to have heard the voices. Julie touched her Amaroq totem and squeezed her eyes tightly shut.

Kapugen came home two days after the storm ended. He had stayed the extra days to give Harry Ulugaq time to recover from the appendicitis operation so he could bring him home.

He was hardly in the door before Julie began to tell the story of Ellen and how she had saved Siku and Far Northland. Kapugen stared at her, not hearing what she was saying.

"You are speaking English," he whispered hoarsely. "You have not spoken it since you came home." She nodded, and her already-rosy cheeks brightened with the excitement of it.

"Then I am forgiven," he said.

"Forgiven?" Julie wondered what made him say that.

"Forgiven for marrying a gussak," he said.

Julie smiled and ran to Ellen and took her hand.

"I love her," she said. "She is my aaka, my mother and my friend."

"I am glad, all right," he said. "I am glad."

"I am glad, all right, too," said Ellen. "I know I am strange to you, Julie, but thank you for those beautiful words."

"Minnesota has fine people," Julie said, and smiled.

"They are fine, all right," Kapugen said, touching Ellen's red curly hair. "Look at this—it is so fine it stands up and curls." Kapugen constantly found her curls a source of wonder. He was quiet as he wound one around his finger.

Julie sensed he had more to say. When Ellen had gone to the bedroom, he walked to the window and back several times. Finally he took Julie's hands in his.

"And am I also forgiven for killing the wolf who saved your life?" he asked.

"How did you know you killed my Amaroq?" she asked after a long pause. "I did not tell you."

"The wolves told me," he replied, and she knew that was true.

Julie blinked and looked at the floor. "It hurts my throat and lungs to speak of Amaroq." She looked up. "But I love you."

"Then I am forgiven?" he asked again. Julie looked into his face a long time as she reached back to the voices of her past. "We do not judge our people," she finally said. "I love you."

Kapugen placed his cold-toughened hands on each of Julie's flushed cheeks and tipped her face until their eyes met. She saw the sorrow he was feeling for her, but she also saw that he would do it again if he had to.

Over their thoughts they heard the spit and chime of running water. Snowmelt was the harmonics. It was tinkling off the roof, out from under the house, down the windows, and over the land to the river. The storm spirit had gone, and the unending sunlight was turning the snow and ice to water. The ocean, the tundra, the rivers were coming out of their frigid straitjackets. Yesterday the ice-stilled Avalik River had buckled with a boom and fractured into millions of pieces. Abetted by water flowing off the tundra, the river had flooded its banks and was hurtling ice and snowmelt seaward toward Kangik and the inlet. The breakup was here.

A moaning roar sounded close by, and above the noise a voice was heard.

"Kapugen! Your boat!"

"Your boat, Kapugen!"

Kapugen rushed out of the house. Julie and Ellen, who had heard and come running, found the ice-filled river almost at the door. It had picked up Kapugen's motor launch and would have carried it away, had not Peter been passing by. He had grabbed it by the bow and was pulling it landward. Kapugen leaped from the doorstep and pulled too, his boots ankle deep in flowing ice and water. Suddenly a house-sized chunk of ice rose like a whale from the river and rolled toward them.

Julie saw she was needed and splashed into the water. She grabbed the gunwale across from Kapugen and she, too, heaved. The boat was jerked landward. Then the huge ice block rose and fell. It created a wave almost as high as a man. Peter saw that it would carry off the boat and wrapped the rope around one of the posts that held Kapugen's house above the per-mafrost.

Julie saw the wave too, let go of the gunwale, and ran, but Kapugen did not. His back was to the wave. It lifted him off his feet, and, losing his grip, he was swirled into the water. Ellen ran to Julie and clung to her in horror as Kapugen was swept away.

Peter grabbed another rope from the boat and ran beside him, looking for a chance to throw it to him. Swimming crosswise to the current, Kapugen was pushed landward.

Ellen covered her eyes. "Dear, baby," she said. "Lie still. Lie still. It will be all right."

Another swell lifted Kapugen high and dumped him on an overturned fishing shed. He clung to it while the wave ran out and back into the river; then he leaped to the beach and ran.

"Nangaun!" he cried in praise, lifting his arms.

Julie did not begin trembling until Kapugen was almost back to them. She hugged Ellen, only to find she was shaking too.

Not Kapugen. He was laughing. His clothes were dripping and his wolverine ruff was wet but not soggy. His hair was plastered against his head. He slapped Peter on the back and said something, and Peter laughed, too.

"Why are they laughing?" Ellen asked in shock.

"You must have a sense of humor to live in the Arctic," Julie said. "Eskimos laugh. It's the best way."

"At prank jokes," Ellen said. "Not at death."

"At death," said Julie. "It's the best way."

Kapugen and Peter pulled the boat far up on shore; then Kapugen changed his clothes and put on his rubber breakup boots. He joined the villagers, who had come running when they heard the river had taken Kapugen and given him back.

Atik and Uma arrived. Uma's little son, Sorqaq, whose English name was Perry, peered over her shoulder. He was inside her amaunnaq, the woman's coat designed to carry babies and toddlers. A belt around Uma's coat at her waist kept Perry from slipping to the ground. He stood up on it and looked out. A wind hit his face, and he slid down against his mother's warm body.

Malek came running, and behind him came Marie, the storekeeper.

"Aaya," Marie said to Kapugen. "You must have offended the spirit of the river. She did not take you." The friends laughed.

Marie was joined by her husband, Ernest Adams, a famous walrus-tusk carver. His grandfather had been a Boston whaling captain who had settled in Wainwright and married AnugI, the best bootmaker on the Arctic coast. It was AnugI's father who had taught Ernest to carve ivory.

Julie studied Ernest Adams, for he was both Eskimo and gussak. His skin was lighter than Marie's and his face more elongated, but he had the dark eyes and broad, high cheekbones of the Eskimos. Ernest's appearance was not exceptional. Many Eskimos had white fathers or grandfathers, and recently some had been born to white mothers. More and more women from the lower forty-eight were coming to the Arctic to teach, practice medicine, and take a variety of jobs. Several, like Ellen, had married native men, stayed, and raised families. Julie looked from Ernest to Ellen's full figure. She was excited about the little child who would soon be among them.

Another woman joined the group, greeting Ellen. Her six-year-old son smiled shyly, and Ellen turned to Julie.

"This is Benjamin, my student," she said. "And Benjamin, this is my daughter, Julie." He smiled shyly at Julie and ran to Kapugen. "I am glad the river gave you back," he said to him.

"You bet," answered Kapugen. "I'm too nasty. It did not want me." Benjamin laughed, picked up a stone, and threw it at the water.

"Bad river," he said. "I punish the river." Kapugen laughed and, picking up the little boy, put him on his shoulders as Peter walked up.

"The water is rising close to your house," Peter

said. "Should we tie ropes to it and try to save it?"

Kapugen jounced Benjamin playfully. "The worst is past," he said, pointing upriver. "When I was flying home this morning, I saw that most of the tundra is snow bare and there are no dams of ice to break loose."

"Did you see the one that brought this flood?"

"I think I did, near duck camp, but I do not know. The one I saw did not look so big. The breakup plays pranks."

The river began to recede, and the villagers were told they were not needed to save Kapugen's house, but no one went home. It was sunny and warm, almost forty degrees. Everyone was happy to be outdoors. A snowbird trilled a cascade of sweet notes, and Julie turned to find him. The bird flew off with seeds in his beak.

"It's summer," exclaimed Julie. "The snowbirds are feeding their babies."

"It's summer," cried Benjamin, and slid down Kapugen's back.

"It's time to celebrate," said Kapugen. "I brought back a big sack of flour from Barrow. We'll make Eskimo doughnuts."

"I have whale meat and maktak," said Malek, who

had just returned from a successful whale hunt. A great cheer went up.

"Maktak," Benjamin shouted, and danced in a circle. "I love maktak better than candy."

"Kangik will have a whale festival, Nalukataq," Malek said. "It is time to share."

"How many whales did Wainwright take?" Atik asked.

"Five. That is their quota this year," Malek said. "It is not enough for everyone, but it cannot be helped. We cannot take more than the whaling commission permits us."

"Why?" shouted Benjamin. "I love lots and lots and lots of maktak."

"We want the whales to live," said Malek, "so that you, your children, and your grandchildren will have maktak."

"And Nalukataq, and blanket tosses," added Marie.

"Where is the blanket?" asked Atik.

"In the back of the store," Marie said. "Come help me get it—everyone come help."

"A blanket toss, a blanket toss," said Benjamin. He met his friend Roy, and together they jumped into one puddle after the other as they made their way down the pebbly street to the church. Other children were running and splashing in every puddle they could find on their way to Nalukataq. It was puddle time for the Arctic children and for Julie. She had on her breakup boots and was standing in a deep pool, kicking water and laughing. Puddles were a rare treat in the Arctic.

Nalukataq was held on the grounds in front of the church. The church was primarily a community center for the villagers, since the minister came to Kangik only a few times a year. Today it had become a community festival ground.

The river roar was a backdrop for the activity. Coleman stoves were set in a circle, and pots of water for cooking put on to boil. Malek pulled his sled of whale meat and blubber into the midst of the cooks and celebrants and cut the long slabs of meat into chunks for the pots. He carved the delicious skin into small bites with a strip of blubber on each—this was the maktak. Then he carved the fluke into thin slices. Taktuk, his wife, would distribute the fluke in a ceremony that some elders said was four thousand years old.

Only about fifty people remained in town, but in less than an hour every house was empty and the festival was in full swing. The sealskin blanket was spread on the ground. Marie served duck soup, and Uma and Taktuk passed out the raw maktak. Four drummers put up a band shell of caribou skins. They tuned up their round flat drums, which were on sticks like lollypops, and sat down on furs, their backs straight. Harry Ulugaq, who was still weak from his operation, was helped to the drum stand. He was determined to play and sing.

The first ponderous beat of the whale-liver-skin drum sounded. It gave a special sound for the opening of Nalukataq. Julie and Ellen hurried home to make the Eskimo doughnuts Kapugen had promised. Julie hung her wet mittens to dry on one of the wooden beams that held Kapugen's kayak near the ceiling.

"How do you make Eskimo doughnuts?" Ellen asked.

"I don't know," Julie said, laughing. "I'll go ask Marie—she should know." She ran off and returned a few moments later, grinning sheepishly.

"You put fifteen handfuls of flour into a bowl with some water and sugar and let it ferment for five days. Then you roll it, cut it, and cook it in deep whale oil."

"Really?" Ellen said, and winked. "Eskimo women have a big sense of humor, too. Let's do it the Minnesota way." She took out a large pot, opened her cookbook, and told Julie to read off the ingredients as she mixed.

Julie read and thumbed through the book between directions.

"What is apple pie?" she asked.

Ellen looked up with a start.

"I thought everyone knew," she said. "I'm always forgetting that I'm in the Arctic. Apple pie is to the lower forty-eight as maktak is to the North Slope. Gussaks love apple pie. They have to, because everyone says they do." She laughed and dumped the mix on the table, patted it, then flattened it out. "When Nalukataq is over, I will bake you an apple pie."

"What are apples?" Julie asked. Ellen threw up her sticky hands.

"I will never get used to no trees," she said. "I still think I can run out in the backyard and pick apples. It's a delicious fruit that grows on a tree." Ellen's eyes glistened, and Julie knew she must be homesick. She remembered how she had felt in Barrow when someone talked about Nunivak. Minnesota was even farther away.

The drums throbbed, and voices rose in rhythmic song. Ellen showed Julie how to cut the flattened dough into round circles with a drinking glass and put a hole in the center with the mouth of an empty pop bottle. After she tested the oil, they dropped in the doughnuts three at a time.

"When they are brown, lift them out with this strainer," Ellen said. She began opening cans and mixing an enormous bean salad.

Kapugen came in to get his Eskimo yo-yos, two fur-covered bags on two strings, for the yo-yo contest and picked up a doughnut cooling on the rack. He turned it curiously.

"Minnesota doughnut," said Julie. Kapugen took a big bite, said "Ummmm," and took another.

"This needs salmon to make it really good," he said.

"Salmon?" said Ellen, horrified, but Kapugen did not hear. He had hurried outside and opened his game cellar, a twelve-foot-deep square hole in the permafrost. He climbed down the ladder into the eighteen-degree atmosphere and came back into the house with three huge salmon.

"And now to celebrate the great whale," he said, putting the fish in a bag and slinging it over his shoulder. Julie carried the doughnuts in a large bucket, and Ellen brought the salad. The Kapugen family joined the celebrants to the beat of the tundra drums.

When the villagers had gathered, Taktuk stood on her family's sled.

"Anyone here have a husband and three children?" she called.

"Me," called Marie, and ran forward laughing.

"A precious piece of the flipper for Marie," Taktuk said, handing her a prized morsel. Everyone clapped as Marie ran back to her stove.

"Anyone here with a gold tooth?" Taktuk called.

"Henry, Henry Smith," everyone shouted, and pushed a nimble little man into the center of the circle. Taktuk called for many more people by spouses, numbers of children, color of parkas, sizes of breakup boots.

"One more piece," she finally called. "Anyone here who loves Kapugen's Julie?"

"I do," a young man called instantly.

"I do," Kapugen and Ellen called simultaneously, but too late. Peter Sugluk was dancing out into the circle to claim the prize.

The schoolboys leaped and laughed and the girls giggled. The adults smiled and told jokes. Julie stepped behind Kapugen and buried her face in his attigi, the summer parka, then peered around him.

Peter took his large slab of flipper and, holding it

high, walked over to Ellen and presented it to her. He was dressed in his traditional clothing, a reindeer parka with wolverine trim.

Peter bent his knees, took a wide stance, and stamped his toe. The drummers picked up his rhythm as he danced into the center of the circle.

Peter danced lightly and gracefully. He held his arms out as he beat a complicated rhythm with toes, arms, and body. He shot an imaginary spear into the sky. He skinned a mysterious animal, scraped it, and wrapped it around his shoulders. He moved so nimbly, he seemed more like a fox hunting in the snow than a person. Finally he stopped and bowed to the villagers.

"As you know," he said in Yupik, "I am grateful to my adopted parents, Malek and Taktuk. I now dance for them."

Peter danced like a reindeer coming across the tundra, like a flock of snow geese speeding over the sea ice, like a seal, like a whale, like a herd of caribou. His hands, feet, and body were as graceful as the ivory gull. No one had ever seen such dancing before, and they watched with rapt attention, Julie among them.

Then he beckoned to her. She hesitated. Kapugen urged her into the circle, and with a smile she began to dance. She held up her hands, wrists bent, thumbs tucked, and danced while Peter's feet kept time. She danced a woman's dance she had learned in Nunivak. When her dance was done, she bowed and Peter performed another man's dance, ending it with swift, complicated footwork. Then he walked over to Julie as if to claim her.

"Where did you learn the dance?" Julie asked shyly. "It's very wonderful."

"Siberia," he said. "That is my home."

"Siberia?" Julie at last knew why his accent was different. He came from far away. "How did you get here?" she asked. He took her arm and walked with her to the blanket for the blanket toss.

"With the Siberian Yupik Dancers," he said. "We have been dancing in Barrow and Kaktovik in Alaska and Kraulshavn in Greenland. I come from Provideniya, Siberia. We are all one people, you know, we who live around the North Pole. I speak Yupik. You speak Yupik. We hunt and fish. You hunt and fish. Nations make borders, cultures do not. I am here and we're dancing the same steps although we never met before." He leaned over and picked up a side of the blanket. Julie took a firm grip, as did the other villagers.

"Where are your dancing friends?" she asked

when everyone had a place around the sealskin blanket.

"They have gone home. Our visiting time was up. I liked it here. One day I met Malek. He told me Kangik had musk oxen and that he needed help with them.

"I told him I knew about them. We have musk oxen on our side of the Arctic Ocean, too. So that I could stay, Malek and Taktuk legally adopted me, and I have been very happy."

"Siberia," Julie repeated.

"We Eskimos were cut off from each other by the white man's politics for so long," Peter said gripping the blanket more tightly, "that we each forgot the other was there. Not our dances and languages. They remember six thousand years back. It is very exciting."

"Hup, hup," called Kapugen, and the villagers lowered the blanket to the ground so Benjamin could step onto the center of it. Carefully everyone lifted it up, then down, moving the blanket in a rhythm.

"Up!"

Benjamin flew fifteen feet in the air, pumping his feet and moving his arms to keep his balance. He hung in space a moment, a bright figure in a blue parka with white trim, then came pumping down. He hit the leather blanket and went flying up again. Three times he sped up into the blue sky and down. Then everyone rested.

After Benjamin, Edna Ulugak was tossed. She sped like a little bird and made graceful movements with her arms to much cheering. When she was tired, her big brother was tossed.

The blanket toss went on until everyone who wished had flown up and down like a bouncing ball, perfecting their poses and twists at the top of the ride. When there were no more volunteers, the blanket was put away for the night.

Julie gave Peter a Minnesota doughnut. He put it on his finger, danced a doughnut dance, and ate it. "Strange," he said. Marie gave them maktak on paper plates, and they sat down on the ground to eat.

"Yummm," Peter said. "Just like home."

"One thing you will find that is not like home," Julie said, "is that on this side of the Pole we don't say we love someone unless we do."

"We don't either." Peter said. "I love you." He looked at her. "In Siberia we know right away when we're in love. Over here it seems to take longer. Too much white-man influence. American white men wait until they go to school, get a job, have a house. When they are old men, they fall in love."

Chewing on her maktak, Julie thought of Daniel and her marriage to him at thirteen. She thought the white men were right.

The sun dipped low and then started up the sky. It was very late. Noticing that Ellen was packing up, Julie got up to help her. Peter arose.

"Julie," he said, taking her arm and walking her away from the crowd, "I also wanted to talk to you about your wolves."

She cried in terror, "You know about them?"

"I do."

"How? How?" she asked.

"The wolf," he said, as if she should know better than to ask, "speaks to you of friendship."

"Kapu is a wild wolf," she answered tartly. "That's all." She ran toward Ellen.

"Julie." Peter caught up with her and pulled her aside again. "Kapu and his pack killed a musk ox last night."

Julie spun around. "No," she cried. "No, he didn't. He is in Anaktuvuk Pass with the caribou."

"The grizzly knocked down the fence," Peter said softly and slowly. "I drove her far inland with rifle shots in the air. While I was gone, the wolves came in. They were leaving the carcass when I found them.

They ran off. I fixed the fence and waited to see if they would come back. They did not."

"No, Peter, no," Julie cried. "Kapugen will kill them." She ran off a few steps and came back.

"Please don't tell him," she said. "I must do it."

PART II

AMY,
THE WOLF PUP

*J*ulie felt as lost as she had been in the blinding snowstorm. She stood motionless thinking of what Kapu had done. The drummers were putting their drums away, leftover food was being toted home, and sleepy children were being carried off to bed. Kapugen and Ellen were teaching Benjamin, Roy, and little Edna Ulugak the foot and arm movements of the caribou dance, but Julie saw none of this. She could see only the terrible fate of her wolves.

She did not even see Peter, who was walking backward watching her. In the hazy sunlight of one o'clock in the morning he looked as if he had been cast in an orange bronze.

Julie walked to Kapugen's rescued boat and sat down. She stared at the raging river. The water had abated, but huge blocks of ice roiled up, boomed, sank, and reemerged far downstream. The roar of the

breakup was comforting. It was a sound wall that isolated her from the now-sleepy merriment of Kangik. She could concentrate on what to do about her wolves.

Kapu must have puppies now, she thought. He would not go far from them, and so she laid a plan.

Into her consciousness came the crackle of Kapugen's CB.

"White Fox Base," she heard. "This is Wainwright Rescue Base. Do you read me, Kapugen? Over."

Julie sat quietly thinking of Kapu. The call was repeated again before she shook her head and hurried into the house. She flipped on the CB.

"Wainwright Rescue Base, I read you. Kapugen is not here. Over."

"White Fox Base. This is Search and Rescue calling. Emergency. Emergency. Can you get him? Over."

"I will get him. Out." Kapugen was a member of the Search and Rescue Team of the North Slope. He was needed. Julie ran.

She found Kapugen, Ellen, and Uma dancing in the sunlight near the church. The children were gone, and Uma was showing Ellen how to move her feet to perform a special chorus of the woman's dance. Ellen was following her steps with great artistry. Julie ran up to Kapugen.

"Aapa," she said, "Search and Rescue wants you." Kapugen stopped dancing and, taking Ellen's hand, hurried home with her. Julie followed slowly, thinking up words to tell Kapugen about Kapu and the musk ox.

When she entered the house, Kapugen was getting into his flying jacket.

"Not good news," he said. "A lawyer and his wife from Barrow are lost in the sea. Before the storm they headed out in their boat for Kuk Inlet. No word from them since. I am flying out to see if I can find them." He stepped to his CB and flicked it on.

"Malek," he said into the speaker, "Kapugen speaking. Do you hear me?" A pause.

"I hear you, Kapugen, but not too good. I am sleepy. Over."

"Clear your head, my good co-pilot," he said, "and meet me at the Quonset. Two people are missing in the sea. Out."

He snapped off the radio, kissed Ellen, and patted Julie's cheek.

"I'll be back," he said.

"Aapa." Julie ran to the door with him. "I have something I must tell you."

"Later, later," he said, and rushed into the copper sunlight of the small hours of the day.

"He must find them," Ellen said to Julie's back. "This country has more than its share of tragedies."

"That is how it is," Julie said, and climbed up on the iglek. Ellen went into her bedroom and pulled the blinds so she could sleep. The dogs barked, Kapugen's airplane took off, and Kangik was quiet. Nalukataq was over.

Kapugen was gone two days. When he returned, he was somber and thoughtful. He stopped by the store to tell Marie and a few shoppers that he had located the boat upside down on a lonely beach. It was empty. The lawyer's log book said he had turned around when he saw the storm that had trapped Julie and Ellen. It overtook him. The shoppers shook their heads at the news. They knew what Hilla, the weather spirit, could do, and they were saddened.

For the next week Kapugen was in and out of the house and too busy to either talk to Julie or go to the corral. He and Malek flew back and forth to Barrow on legal matters for the lawyer's family and over the lonely beaches and capes searching for their bodies. Malek turned over the management of the herd to Peter.

Julie waited for a chance to speak to Kapugen. She read some new books she had found when she had helped Ellen clean the schoolroom for the summer. She fished, fed the dogs, and checked the corral fence. In the late afternoon she would go out on the tundra and note the tracks of the mammals and the activities of the birds. She was practicing for the plan she had devised.

The uminmaks were shedding great swatches of qivit as the season changed. Peter came by the house to ask Julie to help him gather it. She accepted, eager to fill in the time until she could speak to Kapugen. When they were done, she would go out on the tundra and listen for messages from her wolves.

Two calves were born one afternoon, and Julie ran all the way home, her black hair flying behind.

"Ellen," she said with great excitement, "Far Northland has two new friends."

"Two more oxen," Ellen said, smiling. "Very good. Very good. We will soon have a herd large enough to make this industry pay for itself." She opened the record book and wrote down the births. "Were they girls or boys?"

"They are both females," Julie replied.

"Good. That means more little ones."

"Let's celebrate," said Julie. "I will catch you a chum, the best salmon. They are beginning to come up the river from the sea."

"Splendid," said Ellen. "I'll cook it the Minnesota way."

It did not take Julie long to catch the fish. She filleted it with deft movements, then watched Ellen stuff it with herbs and dried fruit her mother had sent.

"Julie," Ellen said, straightening up after placing the fish in the oven, "I've been noticing the books you are reading. You are much too advanced to go to school in Kangik next winter."

"I am?" Julie said. "That's too bad. I would like to be a student here."

"You can be a student," Ellen said, "but not here. In a year or so the North Slope Borough will build a high school in Kangik, but until they do, the borough sends Kangik high school students to Barrow, Anchorage, or Fairbanks. You can then go on to the University of Alaska or even to the lower forty-eight to colleges and universities there."

Julie listened attentively.

"If you are interested," Ellen said, "I will get an application for you."

"I will think about it," Julie replied without enthusiasm.

"You would not be alone," Ellen urged. "There would be other young Eskimos your age. You would go to dances and basketball and volleyball games."

Julie was quiet. Ellen tried harder.

"One of my students graduated from the Anchorage high school last year. He will go to the University of Alaska in Fairbanks this fall. Wouldn't that be fun?"

"What do the students do after they are educated?" Julie asked.

"Most come back to the North Slope," Ellen replied. "One is now the Superintendent of Schools. Another is a banker. Another from Barrow is an expert on the Iñupiat language and she's even compiled an Iñupiat dictionary. There is a lot to be done with an education up here. The Eskimo want to keep their culture and at the same time learn more modern skills like using computers and libraries."

Julie sat as still as a hunted rabbit. A week and a half ago she would probably have asked Ellen to get her an application. Today she could not. She had a contract with her wolves. She must save them.

Ellen turned on her symphonic music. She served the salmon.

"Shall I apply for you?" she asked.

"I must think." Ellen, sensing Julie was up against some emotional wall, walked over to the calendar.

"Your little brother or sister will be with us on

the fifth of July, the doctor says. We'll talk about school after the baby comes." They ate quietly, listening to the wind rattling the windows accompanied by Ellen's music.

"Ellen," Julie finally said, "I am very selfish. I have not made a present for my little paipiuraq." She scraped the dishes and put them in a pan of dishwater.

"I sew well," she went on. "I once made beautiful parkas for Nusan, the wife of Kapugen's serious partner." Julie pulled on her rubber breakup boots. "I'll wash the dishes when I come back. I want to go to the Quonset. Kapugen gave me his white ermines. He said they were for me. He said he wanted me to make something beautiful for myself out of them. But I am going to make the baby a glistening white parka of ermine." She put on her attigi. "I am not so selfish anymore," she said.

"You have never been selfish," Ellen replied.

Julie smiled shyly and hurried outside into the cool sunshine. A soft wind was blowing from the distant ocean. The tiny sedges and reeds along the river were sheltering geese and ducks on their nests. Out on Kuk Inlet, now a deep blue-green, men and women in fishing boats were catching the first salmon and whitefish that were on their way inland to spawn and lay eggs. The whale, duck, and seal seasons were over; the fishing season had begun.

Splashing through the mud puddles, Julie designed the ermine parka in her head as she skipped and ran to the Quonset. She did not see Peter until she was almost upon him.

"Julie," he said, smiling. "I was coming to find you. I saw your wolves."

She stopped still. Her eyes did the speaking: *Where?* they asked.

"About forty miles up the Avalik," he answered. "They were carrying food."

"Good. That means they are feeding a mother. They are at a den."

"That's what I thought."

"How many adults did you see?"

"Three."

"Three," she said. "Do you think you saw them all? Atik saw eight in the winter."

"The winter has been hard on wolves. No food. Some have probably starved."

She bit her lip. "I must go to them. Forty miles is not far enough for a wolf. They will be back for another musk ox." She started to leave.

"Can you join me at the shelter?" he asked. "The fourth calf is about to be born, and the cow is acting strangely."

"I will join you later in the day," she said. "I am on my way to get ermine from Kapugen's fur pile in the Quonset. I am going to make Ellen's baby a beautiful coat."

Peter smiled and looked at her over the top of his dark glasses.

"I love you," he said. "Do you love me?"

"Peter Sugluk," she said. "I must finish high school and college and get a master's degree in Yupik and Iñupiat before I can think of being in love."

"Has Ellen been talking to you?"

"She has."

"Ellen has been talking to me also," Peter said. "I have applied to the University of Alaska."

"You are going to school?" Julie asked, and laughed. "You are full of surprises." She put her hands on her hips. "I don't know what to think about you."

"Yes, you do," he said, taking her around the waist and swinging her off her feet. He circled twice before he put her down facing the Quonset.

"Now go get the ermine for the baby present," he said. "I'll meet you at the shelter."

Julie caught her balance, then ran around the church and up the trail to the Quonset. Stepping inside, she peered back at Peter. His white attigi flapped as he ran. He was a gyrfalcon speeding to its roost.

I like him, Julie said to herself. *That's all.* But she did not take her eyes away from him until he was out of sight.

It was midnight. The plane engine droned off in the distance, grew louder and lower, and finally cut out. Julie listened from her iglek and waited. Kapugen and Ellen were returning from the doctor in Barrow. Julie had not slept since the midnight sun had colored the tundra orange, for this was the day she would tell Kapugen that Kapu had killed a musk ox. Almost a week had passed since the incident. She was frightened but determined.

Ellen came in the door first and passed the iglek on tiptoes, assuming Julie was asleep. She crossed the room in her stocking feet, winding her red hair on the top of her head. When it was all pulled up and tied, she dipped a pan of water from the thirty-gallon plastic container beside the refrigerator. Ellen took a long drink of cold, fresh river water. Since the breakup the people of Kangik could once again dip their water from the Avalik.

Ellen brushed her teeth over an enamel basin and threw the water down the kitchen sink. At last she went into the bedroom.

Julie listened to the water run down the sink pipe and splash on the ground under the house. She heard it trickle away. This was a sound of summer. The sink water was no longer freezing in a glass cone under the house.

Kapugen opened the doors and came in. Julie wiggled to the edge of the iglek.

"Aapa," she whispered, "I have something to tell you." She was almost eye to eye with him.

"Ee-lie, pretty Miyax," he said, and winked. "So you have a love?"

"Aapa," she said, ignoring him. "Please be serious."

"Ee-lie," he said, and kissed her cheek. "Is it that you want to get married?" He brushed back a strand of her hair.

"Aapa, Aapa." Julie slid off the iglek and stood before him. "I want you to listen to what I have to tell you with a soft heart."

Kapugen looked puzzled. "Don't I always?"

"The wolves killed an ox."

The cheerful twinkle left Kapugen's eyes. After a thoughtful silence he turned and went into the qanitchaq. He put on his flying jacket and picked up his wolf gun.

"Please don't," Julie begged. She followed him

into the two-A.M. sunlight.

"Please don't," she pled again.

"It cannot be helped," he answered, taking the path to the Quonset and his airplane. "We need the musk oxen."

"Please, Kapugen, my aapa." Julie ran beside him in her bare feet. "I will keep the wolves away from the oxen. Please do not shoot them. They saved my life." She stopped and reached out her arms to him.

"It cannot be helped," he repeated, but his pace did slow. Julie's eyes filled with tears. She hurried to catch up with him.

"Please, Aapa, it will never happen again. It will never happen again. I know what to do."

"Perhaps the killers are not the wolves who saved you," Kapugen said, wanting to believe this, although he knew there was only one pack between Wainwright and the mountains.

"They are. Don't shoot them," she answered. "Peter saw the pack. One was silver and one was gray. The leader was black."

"But I shot your black leader."

"The black one is his pup. You shot him, too, but not badly. I nursed him back to health." She hesitated. "I named him after you. His name is Kapu. He is a great leader."

"The musk oxen must live," said Kapugen. "We need money for the villagers."

"Atik has walrus, Malek has whale. Duck and goose eggs are everywhere in the river reeds. The whitefish and salmon are beginning their runs."

"We cannot hunt forever," said Kapugen. "The wild animals are passing off the earth. We must find a new way to live in the Arctic. Industry. The musk oxen are our industry."

Kapugen had slowed his pace to a hesitant walk. His face reflected such sadness that Julie could not bear to look at him.

"It cannot be helped," he said once more. "I must shoot the wolves that killed the ox."

"Let me go to them," she said. "I know what to do. You once talked to the wolves. Like you, I learned their language when I was with them on the tundra. I will tell them where the caribou are and send them off to find them. They will do that."

Kapugen ran his weather-darkened fingers over his brow, as if changing his mind. Then his resolve returned and he strode on toward the Quonset. Julie ran after him.

"Please, let me try," she begged. "If I don't succeed, then I will understand. Please, Aapa."

Kapugen let her catch up to him. "In Minnesota,"

he said, "the wolves are protected. No one can shoot them.

"They roam the forests taking deer and moose and an animal they call the beaver. But when a wolf comes onto a person's land and kills his cattle, then the government environmental officers come and shoot him. They shoot the ones that compete with humans. They think that is fair. That is how it is between humans and wolves in Minnesota."

"But not here," Julie said. "We are different. We know the wolf is from the earth and must live so we all can live."

"Not when we live as the white men do." Kapugen had stopped walking. "Eskimos," he said, his voice low as he paced his words carefully, "now live by the Minnesota rules."

"The old rules are best," said Julie.

"I taught you that, didn't I?"

"You taught me that, Aapa."

"I was wrong."

Slender clouds were forming over the bay as the sun began its endless circle around the top of the world again. Julie and her father noted them, as they noted all clouds.

"Sunshine," said Julie. "I can travel."

"Then you will go to them?" Kapugen said quietly.

"I will go to them."

"And what will you do?"

"I do not quite know until I talk to them."

"How will you travel? You cannot take the dogs."

"On foot, until I find them. Then I will travel as they travel." She dropped to her hands and feet and pranced lightly around Kapugen, whimpering and whining like a wolf.

"You did learn their language," he said, pulling her gently to her feet. "Go to them. I know your efforts will be wasted. Wolves do not know about people's property. They see their rightful prey and take it. Wolves have to be wolves."

"Wolves know about borders," Julie said. "They have hunting lands like we do. They mark and patrol them. It is too bad that our musk oxen are on Kapu's land. He thinks they are his."

Kapugen put the gun sling around his neck and let the rifle hang on his back.

"It is useless," he said.

"You will let me try?" she asked.

"I cannot refuse," he said, touching her shiny black hair with the gentleness of a wolf with a puppy. "I will let you try." He rose on his toes, then rocked back on his heels. "If they kill again, I must go by the Minnesota rules."

"All right," she said. "But you will not have to." She wiped her eyes with a knuckle and thanked him with a teary smile.

Kapugen slipped his arm around her shoulder and they walked back home, casting long purple shadows before them.

"Take your .22," he said as they approached the house. "I will give you ammunition."

"I do not want my .22." She remembered the gun blasts that had killed Amaroq and the fear her wolves harbored for guns.

"There are grizzly bears out there," Kapugen went on. "Shoot the gun in the air. It will scare them."

Julie nodded. "Maybe I will take it," she said, recalling the grizzly who had attacked her. Had it not been for Amaroq and his pack, she might not be here now.

Kapugen said no more until he put his hand on the qanitchaq doorknob.

"I will come for you," he said. "My old dog CB will pick up your trail and lead me to you. He's a good tracker, all right. He can smell a seal four miles away and go find it."

"Give me two weeks," she said. "Enough time to get through to them." Kapugen nodded once. He understood. One had to be patient with the Arctic.

Julie spent the next few hours provisioning herself for the trip. She took food, her ulu bag and whale oil, and a change of clothing. She hummed as she made her preparations. She was looking forward to walking in freedom on the open tundra again. This time she would walk without fear of starvation.

When she was packed, she went outside and tacked the white ermines to a board. Carefully she cut them into strips with her ulu. She sat down and stitched them into a single beautiful hide. All the glistening guard hairs lay in one direction. She held up the block of fur and drew in her breath. The ermine bunting was going to be breathtakingly beautiful. She wrapped it around her shoulders, then ran to Ellen's mirror above the kitchen sink. The ice-white fur made her soft olive skin glow and her black eyes more lustrous. She carried it to the iglek and tucked it under the grizzly skin. She would complete the bunting when the baby was born. That would bring the child good luck. She lay down on the iglek and slept.

Hours later, her pack on her back, she stepped outside. She had read the clouds correctly. The air was clear, the sky cloudless. The horizon shimmered.

At least this part of the three-month-long day was going to be beautiful. She walked to the river trail. There she took the totem of Amaroq out of her pocket and held it against her cheek. Then she started off on her journey.

As she approached the corral, she saw Peter and called to him. He waved and came running to greet her. His wide smile clearly said he was glad to see her.

"The calf is born," he called. "Another girl."

Julie smiled, but she did not comment. She had but one thought on her mind.

"Tell me again, Peter Sugluk," she said. "Where did you last see the wolves?"

Peter described an elbow bend in the river and a long beach of white stones. "I saw them walking there."

"Were there any pretty flowers around?" she asked.

"Ee-lie, come to think of it, there were. Why do you ask?"

"Silver likes flowers around her den. They might be denning somewhere near flowers. Were the banks high?"

"They were."

"They like to den high so they can look out over the land."

Peter folded his arms on his chest and tipped his head. His eyes twinkled appreciatively at her knowledge. Then his expression changed.

"What did Kapugen say?" he asked anxiously.

"That he would let me try to save them," she answered. "He will give me this chance. He must shoot them if they kill again."

"What is your plan?" Peter asked.

"I will take them to the caribou, wherever they are," she said.

"How will you do that?" he asked.

"With wolf reasoning," she answered.

Peter grinned and reached into his attigi pocket. "Take this," he said, handing her a small object that was carved out of walrus-tusk ivory. It hung on a thong.

"It's very nice," she said. "What is it?"

"A ground-squirrel whistle," he answered. "I made it. It will amuse you when you are discouraged." She turned it over in her hand, then put it around her neck.

"A ground-squirrel whistle," she said, ducking her chin and looking up at him with laughing eyes. "I will think of you when I blow it."

"That is what it is really for," he said. "To make you think of me." He folded his arms. "And you *will* think of me when you blow it," he reassured her, and chuckled.

"I am sure I will not be able to help it," she said. "It's a funny gift. A ground-squirrel whistle."

Peter laughed, and his white teeth shone brightly against his bronze skin. The ermine tails on his boots danced.

"I would go with you," he finally said, "but Malek needs me."

"I must go alone," she said. "The wolves are my friends."

Julie looked out across the tundra and pointed her boots toward the wolves.

She stepped lightly around small snow patches as she followed the Avalik River toward its source. Her heels barely touched the ground as she walked. She skipped around poppies and waved to the snow buntings that flew up from the flowers.

A day's walk beyond duck camp, Julie came upon a weasel standing on his hind feet, paws draped on his chest. He was no longer wearing his winter fur of white ermine, but a golden-brown coat that blended with the summer tundra. He was boldly blocking her way. Julie stamped her foot at him. He showed his sharp teeth and screamed but did not run.

Julie walked closer. When she was almost two feet from him, she stopped.

"I am a person," she said. "Why aren't you afraid of me? Is it because you have never seen a human before?" She lifted her arms and swayed from side to side.

"See how big I am?" The weasel twitched his whiskers and stood his ground. "Learn to be afraid of two-legged animals," she said. "They shoot little weasels in the winter and make them into glorious ermine coats." The bright-eyed, pointed-faced weasel stood firm, so she blew him a kiss and went on.

The next day Julie passed a snowy owl on her nest. Like the weasel, the large white bird with its huge golden eyes was not afraid of her. She let Julie come almost up to her fluffy babies before getting up on her feet.

Julie pondered about what she was seeing. The animals were talking to her. The owl and the weasel were saying they were not afraid of people because they rarely saw them. They were saying that Julie was in a wilderness where people did not come. In such country, she knew, the wolves of the Arctic raise their young.

A redpoll flew up from a grassy spot with a piece of fur in her bill. Julie spun around. That was wolf fur. She looked down. The grass had been bent by soft, padded feet, not sharp hoofs. She followed the subtle trail and came upon the sleeping scoop of a wolf. The bits of fur within it were black. Kapu had been here. The trail she was following was his. Her spirits lightened.

Bending low, noting every trampled blade of grass, she traced Kapu's footsteps from his sleeping scoop to an elbow bend in the river. There before her was the white, stony beach Peter had mentioned. The footsteps became lost on the gravel. She went on up-river. Two wolf tracks appeared in the silt, then three, then many, as if wolves were playing. She rounded a bend, and there before her was a high, sandy bank. Scanning it carefully, she located a dark spot—a den. Just above it a garden of yellow poppies bobbed in the wind.

"That's it," she said. She put her pack on a gravel bar in the riverbed where she could clearly see the den and sat down. For several hours she remained absolutely still, not even turning her head.

Nothing moved at the den. But everywhere around it there was great activity. The little birds of the tundra were attending their nests. Longspurs and buntings, redpolls and sandpipers fluttered up and over the riverbank and swiftly back down. Julie continued sitting still. Her plan was going to work. This den was a whelping den, not like the summer nursery with its two exits where she had first met Amaroq and his family. Kapu's pups would still be young, and that was very good.

Carefully, slowly, Julie put up the tent she had made from the caribou Amaroq had felled for her many months ago. Then she spread out her ground skin and lay down to wait for her wolves.

After many hours she heard a wavering cry, then a plaintive whimper. It was Kapu. Her heart beat faster. He walked swiftly along the water's edge. His big feet and long legs were wet with river splash, and his dark body made a bold outline against the sandy bank. He did not see or smell her. He had one thing in mind— the den. He walked directly to it, head and tail held high, fur glistening in the sun, and a wolf smile on his face. He was a glorious animal.

His tail began wagging forty feet from the den entrance and did not stop until he reached it. There he whimpered coaxingly. The white wolf came out. She was not Silver, the mother of Kapu. Julie knew Silver as she knew Kapugen and Ellen. What had become of Silver? Had she succumbed to the food scarcity of the winter and spring?

Before she could think more about this, a fuzzy

pup thrust her nose out of the den and whimpered to her father, then ran up to him. She was black like Kapu. Her nose was short and blunt. She had big paws and a chubby body, and Julie wanted to run to her and pick her up and hug her.

The mother greeted Kapu by licking his cheek; then she pushed her cub back into the den. Julie named the white wolf Aaka, or mother. She named the puppy Amy in honor of her pen pal named Amy. She had been on her way to visit her pen pal when she had become lost and eventually had met Amaroq and his pack on the tundra. "Amy," she whispered to herself as she watched the perky pup. When she got home, she would write her friend and tell her there was a wolf puppy named for her. Amy now had an atiQ, a namesake. She would like that.

Kapu looked up and over the den. He barked the doglike hey-look-who's-coming bark of the wolf. Julie turned her head ever so slightly and saw a third adult wolf trotting home. She immediately recognized Zing, Kapu's brother. He was carrying a ground squirrel in his mouth. Zing leaped over the poppies and dropped it in front of the den, a toy for Amy. For the rest of the summer Amy would be developing her skills with such presents from the tundra.

Zing's presence told Julie a great deal about her old pack. Either Silver had died or Kapu had left her to find a mate and had taken along his good friend and strong brother, Zing. Wolves need partners. One wolf cannot fell big game. Somewhere on the barren tundra the brothers had met Aaka and invited her to join them. Julie imagined the battle for her. It would have been brief. Kapu was bigger and more intelligent than Zing. He would have snarled, showed his canines, even grabbed Zing's ruff. Zing would have dropped to the ground and flashed his white belly fur, the flag of surrender. He would have accepted his defeat, then gotten up and licked Kapu's face. They would have been friends again.

Aaka and Kapu would have mated, and the three would have formed a working pack and traveled their eighty-mile-square territory looking for food. Kapugen's musk ox was an easy take through the broken fence.

Just before the pups were due, all three adult wolves would have dug a den midway up the riverbank. It would be shallow, for it takes Arctic wolves years to dig a deep den in the stonelike permafrost.

Julie wondered about the number of puppies. When food is scarce, wolves give birth to fewer pups; sometimes none at all if they are starving. She did not think there could be many this year, and she was soon proven right. When Aaka came out of the den to stretch and take a swift, exhilarating run, Julie could see to the back and bottom of this first-year den. There was only one puppy. The winter had been hard on the wolves as well as the villagers of Kangik.

Zing approached Aaka but was turned back by Kapu. He stood over him, head up, one canine tooth bared, a friendly reminder to his brother that Aaka was his. "Keep your distance," he was saying, and Zing lowered his ears and tail and walked off.

The wind shifted and Kapu lifted his nose toward the riverbed. Cocking his head to one side, he sniffed. He sniffed again. With that his ears shot forward. He smelled Julie. She moved and he saw her. For a moment he stared; then, wagging his tail furiously, he pulled back his lips in a smile and spanked the ground with both front feet.

"Kapu," she called, "you remember me." With her mouth open she whimpered to show him how happy she was that he had not forgotten her.

Kapu romped toward her, then stopped. He threw back his head and howled a long melodious note that began with a bear's growl and rose to a wind scream. He was saying a pack member was here. Julie howled, harmonizing with him. Zing now saw her and lifted his black lip over one canine tooth and growled.

"Zing, it's me," Julie said, and whined her love for him. Zing wagged his tail. He ran to her and, looking straight in her eyes, said she was family and welcome.

Kapu became excited. He sped like a sea eagle down the beach and back to Julie. She threw him her mitten. He caught it, tossed it in the air, and caught it again. He ran in circles and dropped it. Julie laughed and picked it up. Kapu had not lost his sense of humor even though he was a father and the leader of his pack.

Zing circled Julie several times, then lay down near her. He turned his head and half closed his eyes, saying all was well with him. His strange sister was back. Kapu let himself down on his belly in front of her and crossed his paws. He stared at the mitten. Julie hid it. Kapu lifted his head and threw his ears up and forward. He wanted the mitten. He arose and stood above her, trying to pull rank. Julie laughed and threw it to him.

No more adult wolves joined the pack, nor did any more pups appear. There were only two adults to do the hunting, Kapu and Zing. Aaka must guard her pup. The story was there for Julie to read. The other members of the original group had either joined distant packs or started their own as Kapu had done. Or they were dead—the life of a wolf is dangerous.

The sun circled the top of the world twice, and with each swing Julie moved closer to the den. Kapu and Zing did not care, but Aaka did. She became nervous every time Julie inched her way forward. She growled and bared her teeth. Julie tossed her a mitten, but Aaka would not play. She was proving to be a problem—and she was the most important wolf in Julie's plan. She must get Aaka's confidence if she was going to help her wolves.

Julie was patient. She moved back a few yards and quietly went about a routine of eating and sleeping and waiting. On the fifth morning Kapu scooped a sleeping bed four feet from Julie's tent. He circled and circled, then lay down and went to sleep.

Aaka watched this from the den entrance. After a long time she came down the embankment and walked over to Kapu. She lay down beside him and rested her head on his back. She watched the river out of her cool yellow-brown eyes. Finally she twitched her ears and glanced at Julie. Julie looked at her. Aaka looked away. Julie looked away, but sneaked a glance out of the corner of her eyes. Slowly, thoughtfully, Aaka turned her head and looked right into Julie's eyes. She did not look away. Julie's heart ached with happiness. By looking in her eyes, Aaka was saying she had accepted Julie into the family. Everything was going to be all right.

From that moment on Aaka stopped growling at Julie, and after the next sleep Julie moved her tent almost up to the den door. Aaka made friends with her but would not let Amy come out and play. That was the next problem. Julie needed not only Aaka's friendship but Amy's.

During this time Kapu and Zing were gone long hours hunting for ground squirrels, snowshoe hare, foxes, ptarmigan—anything they could find. One hunt lasted so long, Julie feared Kapu and Zing had gone back to the corral for a musk ox. She was greatly relieved when they returned with a snowshoe hare for Aaka.

In the middle of the next sunny night Julie was awakened by the whimperings and woofs of the wolves. Kapu had dragged a calf carcass to the den, and they were discussing it in their mysterious way. The carcass was so old and battered that Julie was not sure what it was, but it looked to her like a caribou calf.

She was excited. If there was a little calf, the caribou herd could not be far away. Later in the sunny night, when the wolves had abandoned the carcass, Julie looked at it closely. The animal wore a radio collar around its neck like the one Atik had described.

She took it off and cleaned it in the river. A tag on it read: Return to Alaska Fish and Game Department, Fairbanks, AK. She put it in her pack. She would do that.

Another day passed and Julie still could not get close to Amy. The mother wolf was keeping her pup hidden even though she herself was comfortable with Julie. Julie wondered why, but then she remembered that wolves did not think like people. They thought with scents and sounds as well as vision. This left them either completely disconnected or, if they chose, so alert they could sense aggression. She decided that Aaka was being alert and had read her plan in her face or eyes—and did not like it.

Julie thought about how to get Amy to be her friend. It was absolutely essential to her next move that the little pup trust her. She was thinking about what to do when Aaka sat down beside her. Julie whimpered pleasantly to her. Aaka whimpered, then turned and looked back at the den. Amy was sitting out in the open under the poppies. Julie whimpered. The little pup got up and ran to her. She grabbed her boot thong and tugged, growling ferociously while wagging her tail. Then she looked at Julie and spanked the ground with her forepaws to say, "Let's play." She longed to pick up the adorable pup, but Aaka's eyes said she was not ready for that.

Amy woofed. Julie woofed back. She held out a bone from the caribou carcass. Amy grabbed it in her teeth and pulled. She growled joyfully, pulling harder, then let go. Julie fell backward. After another game of tug-of-war and one game of boneball, Aaka got up and led Amy back to the den. But a great barrier had been crossed. Julie closed her eyes and breathed with relief. Things were progressing.

The next day when Kapu and Zing went off to hunt, Aaka led Amy to Julie again. Julie picked up the bone and waggled it before Amy, who grabbed and shook it. They tugged and chased while Aaka walked off and stretched out in the sun. She closed her eyes to say she had complete confidence in Julie at last.

"Can I pet you?" Julie whispered to Amy. The pup twisted her head curiously and Julie gently reached out and buried her fingers in the soft fur. She scratched the little head and the pointed ears. Amy closed her eyes and Julie took her hand away. Amy nudged her hand for more scratches. Julie petted her again, then held out the bone. Amy grabbed it, pulled powerfully, and let go. Again Julie went over back-ward, and this time the pup pounced on her. Amy yipping, and Julie laughing, they tumbled on the gravelly beach. Aaka did not lift her head.

After a while Aaka got to her feet, shook, stretched, and yawned. Then, without looking back, she wagged her tail and ran off.

Aaka sped over the tundra like a bird released from a cage. She ran in circles, chased cotton-grass seeds, then disappeared around the bend in the river. Julie got to her feet, her heart pounding, her hopes high. She could see Aaka racing across the tundra tracking Kapu and Zing. Julie saw that she was going to win. Aaka trusted her to be the baby-sitter.

Amy played with a bone for a short while, then crawled into Julie's lap. She whimpered and Julie sang her songs until the little pup sighed and slumped into a deep sleep. Then Julie picked her up and carried her back to the den.

Her baby asleep, Julie got her .22 and walked into the grasses. She wandered for quite a while before she saw a ptarmigan and shot it. This, too, was part of her plan.

When she returned to the den, Amy was awake. She sniffed the bird, shook it, then dropped it and looked at Julie as if to ask what she should do with it.

Julie skinned it and offered her a tasty morsel. Amy licked it, then grabbed it in her sharp teeth and gulped. She came back for more. This time Amy took the bird, which she ate after smashing it, bones and all, with her small but powerful teeth and jaws.

The little wolf decided one wing was a toy. She shook it in Julie's face. When Julie grabbed it, Amy pulled it away and ran in circles. Julie tricked her by flashing the calf bone in one hand. Amy dropped the wing for the bone, and Julie got the wing. With that Amy sat down. She would not play anymore, even when Julie gave her the wing. For the remainder of the time the hunters were away, Amy ignored Julie.

"You didn't like that, did you Amy?" Julie said to her. "You don't like to be tricked. I am sorry." To make up for her error, Julie offered her a piece of dried caribou. Amy looked right through it as if it were not there. She did not even seem to see Julie. *Where does the mind of the wolf go at times like these?* Julie wondered. *Far out on the tundra? Over the river?* She did not know.

The next day Amy was playful again. Whatever had been in her wolf mind was not there today. She left the adult wolves and romped to Julie, chewed her boot thong, and asked to be scratched and petted. When they were as close as sisters, Julie gently, gently

picked her up. The pup cuddled. Julie glanced at
Aaka. She was lying on her side completely uncon-
cerned. Julie was overjoyed. She carried Amy down to
the river. Kapu and Zing awoke, stretched, yawned,
and shook themselves. After a short howl they trotted off to hunt. Aaka went with them, leaving Amy in
Julie's arms. Julie was part of the wolf pack.

When the wolves came home, their bellies were
rounded with food and they slept for a long time.
When they all finally awoke, Kapu inaugurated the
leadership ceremony. He did this each wolf morning.
He stood above Zing, who lowered his head and
licked Kapu's cheeks. Then Kapu mouthed his muzzle and shook it gently. Aaka approached him, ears
down, head down, and he lifted his head above hers.
She licked him under the chin and along his neck to
tell him he was a fine leader. Kapu, like all wolf leaders, needed lots of reassurance from his pack. Having
gotten it, he trotted to the highest point on the embankment, poised himself, and howled. Zing and
Aaka howled. Amy yipped. They sang their music for
many minutes. During the concert, the noisy birds
quieted down and the ground squirrels retired to
their elaborate underground tunnels and dens. When
they were done, Zing turned to Aaka and seized her
muzzle to tell her he had more status than she did.

She quickly corrected that.

That evening when the hunters were gone, Julie put Amy in her backpack and carried her along the riverside to find another bird to eat. The wolf pup did not try to get out of the pack; rather, she peered around at the world, seemingly pleased with her high seat. Julie walked a long distance without finding anything and was starting back to the den when a ground squirrel dove into one of the many entrances into his underground city.

"Peter," she said, "I'm thinking of you." And she pulled the whistle out of her shirt and blew it.

Eeekk-chirp. Two ground squirrels poked their heads out of the burrow. She blew it again. Three more appeared. The more she blew, the more little squirrels appeared. Amy yipped and Julie put her down on the ground. She blew the whistle again; another head popped up. The little wolf pup pounced, and all the ground squirrels disappeared.

"What a special gift, Peter," she said, and laughed right out loud. "This will come in very handy."

When Kapu, Aaka, and Zing came home, this time with their stomachs empty, Julie walked to the ground-squirrel colony and blew the whistle. Up came the ground squirrels. The wolves saw, wagged their tails, and gobbled.

"Ee-lie, Kapu," she said when he had eaten his fill, "it is time to move on."

The clouds were sailing in a marine-blue sky. The birds were flying to nests of hungry babies. Julie packed her belongings.

She picked up Amy and put her in the pack. When Julie had reached the top of the embankment above the den, Aaka opened her eyes. Julie walked on. Aaka got to her feet. She sensed a new attitude in Julie. Kapu awoke. Zing stood up. They all watched Julie walk south with Amy in her pack. Aaka trotted right after them. Kapu followed, then Zing.

Their pup was going somewhere, and they were going with her.

Julie turned to her friends. "We are going on a long walk to the mountains," she said. "The caribou are there. You can eat your fill."

She walked faster. Kapu, Aaka, and Zing walked faster.

At first Julie thought the white blazes on the horizon were sunlit clouds, but as she walked on they became more solid and she realized she was looking at the splendorous Brooks Mountain Range. She stopped to rest and take in the spiritual force of the mountains; then she proceeded on south toward the Colville River.

All the while she walked she sang "The Far Northland" and "Peas That Go *Tink*, Peas That Go *Tot*," a song she had made up last year on the tundra. Amy and her somber line of relatives seemed to listen and smile at her music. Occasionally a tail wagged when she sang a sour note.

She looked for caribou droppings and their hoofprints. The prints would be half circles, split in the middle and about five inches long. Dewclaws on the front feet would leave two dots behind each track. She saw no caribou sign.

The wolf pack patiently followed their pup. They were not much concerned about why Amy was in the backpack. She was in view, and that was all that mattered. They trotted along looking at the scenery and sniffing the air.

Kapu occasionally made a wide circuit to search for game. He had been over this ground many times. He and his pack, like other wolves of the Arctic, knew every pond, grass clump, and large animal on their huge territories. Kapu could inspect a vast swatch of tundra with his nose, for he could smell game more than ten miles away.

Julie was glad for Kapu's all-seeing sense of smell. The herd had to be somewhere nearby. A calf does not wander far from its mother, and Kapu's nose could "see" them long before her eyes. She hurried along.

Amy rode quietly in the backpack. The pup was young enough to heed the voice of authority. A growl, a snarl, or a snappy bark from Julie, and Amy would stop chewing her way out of the pack and lie still.

The strange party covered almost thirty miles in one sun orbit before they stopped to sleep. The wolves were not tired, but Julie was. She sat down with a thump on a warm, grassy hummock and stretched out her legs. She chewed on caribou jerky and felt the permanence of the mountains that rose so high above her. Among the lines of dark-green trees dwelled the wild things. They lived out their lives there, had young, and lived on. She liked the nurturing mountains.

At her feet the little birds chirped, dipped, and flew around her, reminding her of a snowstorm. The mosquitoes hummed but did not bite. She was odorless to the big Arctic mosquito. A smaller one would plague her when she reached the Colville unless she covered herself with fish oil, which she had remembered to bring.

Julie had settled down, but the wolves were restless. They paced back and forth, sniffing and twisting their ears. After a while they lay down, ears up.

When they seemed to be settled, Julie took Amy out of the pack and gave her to Aaka to nurse. But Aaka could not provide much milk. She had not eaten well for months. After a few frustrating suckles, Amy gave up. She looked around for Kapu and poked her nose into the corner of his mouth to ask for food. The stomach basket was empty. He had nothing to give. Amy whimpered in pain, and Julie got to her feet, loaded her .22, and kicked through the grasses.

She came back with a snowshoe hare and gave it to Aaka, who tore it apart and shared it with Amy. Kapu and Zing slept to conserve energy.

Julie joined the sleep. She put down her caribou skin and was dreaming before she could take off her boots. Hours later she was awakened by the plaintive cry of a peregrine falcon. She sat up. Peregrines feed largely on ducks and geese. Ducks and geese live by water. The voice of the peregrine told her she and her wolves were near the Colville River—and caribou.

Suddenly the falcon folded its wings and plummeted earthward. A puff of feathers spiraled into the air, and Julie rolled to her knees. Kapu lifted his head, sniffed, and leaped to his feet. He raced toward the falcon's kill. The falcon beat her wings as Kapu approached and took off, leaving the goose. Kapu walked up to it and took it in his mouth. Then he dropped it and came jogging back to camp. He lay down and glanced at each member of his pack to say, "I didn't take it—don't you."

The peregrine circled back. She had seen Kapu walk away from her meal and lie down. When he was very still, she dropped like a meteor upon her kill. Taking it in her talons, she beat her strong wings and soared away.

"Why did you do that, Kapu?" Julie asked. "Why did you leave the goose? You've barely eaten anything for days, yet you gave the food to the falcon." Kapu's eyes softened. He looked at Julie, then stretched out on his side and watched the sky.

"Kapu," Julie whispered on, "do you know what the Eskimo knows? Did you let the peregrine falcon eat and live because the tundra community needs falcons? Is that why you did not take her food? I believe so. The elders say the wolf sacrifices not only for its family, but for the whole environment."

Julie got to her feet, put Amy in her pack, and went on. Aaka followed close behind the two. Kapu and Zing circled out and back as they moved along, always keeping that pup in sight, as if pups were the only thing wolves lived for. And at this time of year, Julie knew, it was true. Her plan was working.

A few hours later Julie came into the foothills of the Brooks Range. Above them the great snow-covered mountains filled half the sky. Julie had come to the rugged winter home of a western caribou herd. She climbed a knoll to look around. Below her snaked a line of green.

"The Colville River," she exclaimed aloud, and ran down the slope searching for caribou.

But there were no caribou hoofprints. No ladder-like horns clawed the sky.

She sat down to cry, but mostly to think. There seemed to be little point in going on. Yet she must. She had been abroad for eleven sleeps, but the Kangik musk oxen were only a running day away for the wolves. She must get the pack near Anaktuvuk Pass, where Atik had said a few caribou had been seen. The pass was almost two hundred miles away, but she must go. She let Amy out of the backpack to romp and play, shot a ptarmigan for the pup, and took a nap. Then she packed up and walked toward a bluff over the river.

The wolves followed their pup. Their feet moved so smoothly under them, they seemed to float on a sea of wind. Suddenly Kapu stopped. He put his scent on a clump of grass, sprayed a dwarf willow, and ran back to Julie. He scratched a deep blaze on the ground. She shrugged and walked on. The wolves did not follow. Julie whimpered impatiently. Kapu barked.

"Come on, come on," Julie urged. Kapu howled and ran the exact same path he had just run. Zing also ran the line and put his scent on the grass and willow.

Aaka ran the line, returned, and put her front feet on Julie's pack as she reached up to grasp Amy. Julie growled. Aaka cowered. Quickly Julie apologized and hugged the gentle mother wolf.

"We must go on," she said urgently, and started off again. Anatukvuk Pass was ten sleeps away, and Kapugen was probably already on his way to find her. He would locate her quickly with CB tracking her. She did not want that. She must get the wolves to a new food source before she met her father. Determined, she took Amy out of the backpack and carried her in her arms as she headed southeast.

She crossed the invisible line again.

Kapu wolf barked and stood where he was. He would not follow. Zing barked, Aaka whined. Julie walked on. They whimpered and called to Amy, but they would not cross the line. It was as if a huge wall of glass had been erected and they could not go through it. They ran north and south, but not toward the pass. When Amy tried to squirm out of Julie's arms, Aaka trotted over the invisible line to get her. Kapu bark-snarled, lifting his lips to expose not one but both canine teeth. Aaka came back. She did not make another move to get Amy, although Julie was running farther and farther away, determined to make them follow.

They would not. All three stood on the knoll looking at her. Then Kapu lifted his head and howled a deep, lugubrious note. Zing harmonized with him, and Aaka called out a sweet, pained cry. To the wolves their song was about losing loved ones. To Julie it spoke of heartbreak, and she turned back to them.

As she came over the invisible line, tails wagged and wolf tongues licked her hands. She sat down and wondered what to do. Then Kapu got down on his belly and put his head on his forepaws. He stared toward the river bottomlands.

With that Julie finally realized what the three wolves were saying. This invisible line, marked with urine and paw marks, was the end of the pack's territory. One step over and they were breaking a wolf taboo. She was heartsick. She could not reach caribou land with her wolves.

In distress she hugged little Amy, who licked her chin, then looked at her mother. Kapu trotted off a short distance and mouthed Zing's muzzle, then Aaka's. They wagged their tails and lowered their ears and tails as if agreeing with him. Aaka tossed her head and swiveled her ears. Gradually Julie realized an important message was being sent around the wolf pack, but she did not know what it was.

And then they told her. They ran out on the tundra and sped away like bird shadows.

"Humpf," she said aloud. "I'm the baby-sitter again." She hugged furry Amy.

After spreading her caribou skin, she romped in the grass with Amy before giving her a piece of caribou jerky. The pup growled and ate pleasurably. Julie stretched out on her belly.

Chin in her hands, she studied the river. The caribou country beyond was to have been the new home of her pack. Now that could not be. She could not get her wolves to move across the river. Their territory had ended. She had to leave them to their fate.

Julie blinked. There was a deep dent in the sphagnum moss. The pressure of a footfall had forced the water out of the moss and left a hole. She got up and walked to it.

"Moose," she said, standing over a five-inch track. The cloves were not spread as wide apart as those of a caribou, and they were sharper and more elongated. She found many more. They led in and out of the river bottomland. Julie raised her arms in joy. Caribou were wanderers who moved from northern to southern Alaska in a huge continuous circle, but moose were different. A moose rarely moved more than eight miles from its birthing spot.

"Moose," she repeated. "The wolves will live."

But moose live in the bottomlands along rivers, and somehow she had to get her pack over the invisible line and into river bottomland.

Something moved. Julie focused her eyes on the far side of the Colville. Above the ten-foot willow trees a wolf trotted, and Julie realized why her wolves would not go forward. On the other side of the river was another pack. Julie watched them motionlessly.

The silver wolf was joined by a gray wolf. It lifted its leg to scent mark, stating that it was a male. The pair sniffed the air. The wind was carrying Julie's scent to them. They turned their heads looking for her, but were unable to locate her with their eyes. The male sprayed again, then trotted down his invisible border. His line was above moose country too.

What is going on? Julie asked herself. There is a

pack over there and a pack over here and a great space in between that no one will enter. And it is full of moose. She recalled Kapugen telling her that certain Indian tribes set up corridors between their territories where no person could go without fear of death. Over the ages this no-man's-land became a game preserve. Overhunted animals would retreat to the safety corridor and in time recover their numbers. When there were too many deer or moose for the corridor to sustain, they were forced up into Indian land and were harvested again. When the white man changed the land laws, the Indians starved. The wolves, it seemed, had a similar arrangement.

"Now what do I do?" she asked Amy, who had fallen asleep in the sun.

Julie's mind raced. The young ground squirrels were abroad, chattering noisily. The baby birds were out of their nests, catching their own food. The lemmings had many litters, and the weasels, foxes, owls, hawks, and jaegers were feasting. Mobs of white-fronted geese and their young gabbled along the river's edge. July, called Iñukkukaivik, the month when the animals are raising their young, was coming to the Arctic.

Julie lay down by Amy and slept.

Many hours later the three wolves came home

looking well fed, their stomachs round. Amy ran to her mother and stuck her nose into the corner of her mouth, saying, "Food, give me food," and Aaka did. Julie smiled. She had almost starved to death last year, before she had learned how to ask the wolves for food. It was Kapu who had taught her that the parent wolves brought food home to the pups in their bellies and that all one needed to do was to touch the corner of an adult's mouth and the wolf would give it up freely.

The wolves stretched out in the somber sunlight. Julie was glad they had eaten, but she knew well that this meal was only a snack. A grown wolf needed six or seven pounds of food a day. Their ribs were beginning to show through their fur. Time was running out.

And her pack could not get to the moose.

The sun was skimming lower along the horizon each midnight to say darkness would return to the Arctic. It was also saying something else. The light around the sun was a muddy yellow. Julie knew this color well. A very heavy fog was rolling in from the coast. Soon she would not be able to see her feet. Apparently the wolves knew this too, for having eaten all they could find, they were now scratching out beds for a long sleep.

As Kapu circled to lie down, Julie wondered if he knew about the wolves on the other side of the river. She should have known better. With his ears, whiskers, nose, and tail he was constantly monitoring the other pack and reporting their activities to Zing and Aaka. He knew exactly what was going on, and finally told Julie. He stopped making his bed and stared across the river. His fur rose straight up on his head and neck, then on down to the tip of his tail. Julie looked where he was looking. The distant pair was edging over their invisible line. Since they were too far away to hear Kapu growl, he was warning them to go back with ears and neck fur. They saw his threat and backed off. The wolves on the other side of the river walked into the grasses and lay down.

Julie hugged her knees and pondered. A wall of fog now was visible on the horizon. It came silently toward them, a soupy billow that was erasing the landscape. It could last for days, even weeks. She had a new plan.

When her wolves were asleep, she arose. On tiptoes she crossed the invisible line and broke into a run. Kapu was instantly on his feet. He sped to his border but did not make a sound. The mood had changed with Kapu's hair-raising threat.

At the river's edge, Julie noted, the willows and

sedges were clipped by moose teeth; their huge hoof-prints poked the soil everywhere. Lynx scats dotted the grasses, and some flat stones were the tidy latrines of the wolverine.

Still, her wolves would starve. Her .22 rifle could not fell a moose. It could only irritate it to charge. Suddenly she knew what she must do. She must drive a moose to the wolves. Even one would keep them fed for many days, giving her time to think of a plan to break the taboo and get Kapu and his pack into the rich no-wolf's-land.

Quietly she stalked. On both sides of the river wolves watched her. Suddenly Kapu howl-barked frantically and fiercely—a warning. Julie turned. A bull moose was running down upon her.

There was no place to hide. The willows were sparse here and not much higher than she. She was exposed on all sides. The charging bull held his huge rack high. His bell swung under his chin, and the whites of his eyes gleamed. Julie knew better than to turn and run. To all beasts a fleeing animal invites a chase. She must not incite attack.

She did the only thing left to her. She faced him, and when the huge bull was almost upon her, she jumped to one side. He thundered by, unable to turn quickly and strike her. Several hundred feet away he slowed down and turned around.

Then he lowered his rack, dug in his hoofs, and charged again. *Noise,* thought Julie, *make noise.* She threw back her head and howled. Kapu, Zing, and Aaka howled.

The moose halted, flared his nostrils, and looked up the slope. The wolves howled again. He turned and ran. Now Julie felt what all predators feel—the urge to chase the fleeing beast. Howling and shouting, she ran the huge animal out of the river bottomland, up through the willows and onto the foggy tundra. The wolves took up the pursuit.

Her plan had worked. Now she must figure out how to break the taboo. She could not stay in the river bottomland all winter chasing moose out of the no-wolf's-corridor for Kapu.

The only answer was to join the two packs into one.

She took off her boots and waded into the icy river, selecting the shallowest water. The fog bank was still far from the river. Julie judged she had plenty of time to woo the two wolves and find their den. She would make friends with another puppy and carry it into the corridor. Then she would go back and get Amy and bring her into the bottomland. The adults would have to come for them. There probably would be a terrible fight, but Kapu, she was certain, would win. That would make the two new wolves obedient to Kapu. The taboo would be broken. They would hunt the moose in the corridor and not come to Kangik for musk oxen.

She was pushing through the sedges and willows, making plans, when a wolf suddenly appeared before her.

"Silver," Julie said. "Silver, it's you."

Silver looked at Julie and twitched an eyebrow. She seemed to be saying that she was not surprised by her presence, that she had known about her arrival on the Colville for a long time. She wagged her tail once, turned, and trotted off. Julie pranced behind her on all fours. There was another wolf with Silver, and she did not want to threaten him by walking on two feet like a human hunter. A slight rotation of Silver's ears told Julie she was behaving correctly.

They walked among the sedges and dwarf willows, Silver moving like a meandering stream. Julie moved like an Eskimo dancer telling the story of the wolf person who lived before the raven turned the world from dark to light. She also reached in her pocket and rubbed her totem of Amaroq.

Silver stopped to sniff a wolverine print, trotted on a few yards, and sat down. Julie sat down and, whimpering her affection, held out her mitten. Kapu's scent was on the mitten, and Julie hoped it would tell Silver that he was nearby. Silver sniffed the mitten, glanced across the river, then back at the mitten. She was not at all excited by Kapu's scent. Julie understood she knew very well her son was there.

They sat quietly side by side. While Silver cleaned a paw with her tongue, Julie searched the stony riverbank for a den. She could find none, nor did she see any pups appear. Apparently Silver and her new mate had adjusted to the food shortage by not giving birth at all.

Suddenly Silver's mate stood up. Julie swallowed hard. He was no more than ten feet away. The dwarf willows he had been crouched in came only to his white belly. He was large and rangy, his body lean, and his face hard. However, he was smaller than Kapu. That was good. The head of a pack was always the biggest. Kapu would win the fight for leadership if she could get them together. Julie named the rangy wolf Raw Bones. She whimpered, begging his friendship. He ignored her by looking down the river at nothing.

Silver stood up and pushed her rear end toward Julie, lifted her head, and closed her eyes. Julie knew what she wanted. Carefully she reached out and scratched Silver's back just above the tail, where wolves and dogs love to be scratched. Silver growled in pleasure.

"I wish," said Julie wistfully as she dug her nails in and rubbed hard, "that you and Kapu would let each other hunt moose."

Raw Bones took a few steps and stared across the river. Julie followed his glance. Kapu and Zing were standing just back of the invisible border. Their ears and ruffs were up. Their eyes were pinned on Raw Bones. He glared back. Julie thought some great decision was in the making; then Raw Bones suddenly relaxed his gaze, rotated his ears, and stepped closer to Julie. He sniffed her scents as if reading some message she had carried from the other side of the river.

Julie wondered: Had Kapu not called her back because he had marked her with a scent message?

Raw Bones stared across the river and whined the whine of friendship.

Silver bounded forward.

Kapu and Zing leaped over their invisible border and rushed into the bottomland.

Raw Bones and Silver splashed into the river, sending water six feet in the air.

The four met, exchanged signals, and chased a

moose that Julie had not even seen. Back on the tundra stood Aaka and Amy.

The moose knew the call of death. He lifted his huge hoofs and ran effortlessly, rack and head back. The wolves leaped at his side. They circled out and loped back, keeping up with the prey without sound. Kapu signaled with his eyes. The wolves took positions for the kill.

Then Kapu stopped dead in his tracks and so did the others. He had called the hunt off. Panting, lips pulled back in smiles, the four watched the moose for a moment, then turned and trotted away. The moose slowed down, looked back, and as if nothing had happened, lowered his head. He browsed unafraid. The predator and prey, over the millennia, seemed to have worked out some understanding with life and death.

Having chased the moose, the four wolves ran down the gravel shore, ears up, tails flowing behind them. They sped along as if there were nothing more important in the universe than running. Julie was spellbound. They seemed to be performing a ritual of wolfdom. They had not killed the moose, just chased it together. Now they seemed to be running joyously, as if they were celebrating the first law of their kind—cooperation. An elder had put it to Julie another way: "We are all here for each other; the Eskimos, the mammals, the river, the ice, the sun, plants, birds, and fish. Let us celebrate cooperation." That, Julie felt, was just what they were doing.

Through some mysterious signals the wolves had told each other they would join forces and become one pack. And, it seemed to Julie, she had been the messenger. How it had all come to be she did not know.

Julie waded through the sparkling water, put on her boots, and on all fours climbed the embankment to the land that had once belonged only to Kapu and his pack. She looked across the flat landscape to locate the moose she had chased to her pack. It was nowhere to be seen. Apparently it had outrun the wolves, as a moose can do. She did not care. The taboo was broken and there was plenty of wolf food in the bottomland. She was ready to go.

Aaka and Amy did not look at her as she picked up her belongings. They stood perfectly still watching the pack of four agile hunters below them. Then, at some signal from Kapu, Aaka stepped forward and whimpered to Amy, and together they trotted down into the river bottomland.

Julie watched the six wolves sniff and lick each other, wag tails, and discuss wolf matters. That done, they began searching the air with their noses.

"Ceremonies or no ceremonies," Julie said, "they're hungry." She pulled Peter's whistle out of her parka and walked down the slope to a bare hummock where ground squirrels lived. She piped a chitty cry. A squirrel appeared. She blew again. Another rushed out of a burrow and looked around. Raw Bones dashed to the colony. Julie blew many notes. The ground popped with squirrels. Kapu joined Raw Bones. Zing followed Kapu, scaring one down a hole. But the wolves did not catch them. They played with them, chasing them back when Julie whistled them out. Julie laughed. The wolves seemed to be laughing too, as the pipe sounded and the ground squirrels came up. She wondered what note Peter had fashioned to bring the little squirrels out of the ground. Then she remembered how she had waggled her finger last summer on the tundra to imitate the tail signal of the little squirrels' "All's well—no enemies are around, come out." Peter, she realized, had created the ground squirrel's call that also says, "All's well. Come out."

Suddenly the fun was over. Raw Bones was too close to Aaka. Kapu growled at him. Raw Bones bared his teeth back to the molars. Kapu leaped and grabbed him by the scruff of the neck. He shook him and let go. The two snarled as they raised their hackles, showed their teeth, and circled each other. Suddenly Kapu threw Raw Bones to the ground and stood full stature over him, silently showing his canine teeth. Then he stepped back and Raw Bones slunk to his feet, his head lower than Kapu's, his tail almost to the ground. His ears were flattened against his head. The fight for leadership was over. Kapu was the head of the pack. The fog rolled down upon them.

All five adult wolves gathered in a circle and howled. Amy yipped. The song traveled across the river to be echoed back by the cliffs and hills. The song was full of the rightness of the earth. Julie felt the harmony and sang, too.

When a cold wind swept the fog away and revealed the midnight sun, Julie gathered her belongings to go home. A raven winged out of the sky and boldly alighted on her pack. He *quoink*ed, the call of his kind to assemble. Soundlessly, on great black wings, three more ravens appeared, then seven more.

"Wise birds," Julie said. She had not seen a raven since that first day on the tundra. "They know what is going to happen."

A red fox appeared. He had followed the ravens, knowing they could see food from on high. He would share what they found. "But there is no food yet," Julie said aloud, puzzled. Two moose had been chased, but no moose had been felled. The raven and fox knew something she did not. Perhaps, she said to herself, that chorus of wolf voices told the tundra life that there were now five, not just three, adult wolves and they were ready to hunt big game as wolves do.

Julie shouldered her pack and left the Colville. She was satisfied that her wolves had enough game to hold them for many months, perhaps even until the caribou returned. She looked down at her boots, and with a smile she pointed them homeward, toward— she was surprised to admit—Peter Sugluk.

PART III

MIYAX,
THE YOUNG WOMAN

On her homeward walk Julie tracked herself and the wolves back across the tundra. The fog had cleared and she could see the groove in the grasses their caravan had made. In addition, tufts of wolf fur caught on poppy seed heads and grasses were like white flags marking the way.

She had not gone far before she heard the ravens dong the death knell. She stopped to listen. Above the raven anthem rose the voices of the wolves heralding the end of one life and the continuation of others. The moose had given himself to the wolves. She smiled. The musk oxen were safe. If the caribou returned this autumn, Kapugen's industry would go on thriving.

Happily she walked. When weariness overcame her, she lay down on her caribou skin and was quickly asleep. She slept through birdsong and weasel chitter, through wind change and the red-purple cloud

performance at the perigee of the midnight sun.

She was awakened by the wurping laughter of foxes. Four alert pups were dancing around her. Their eyes twinkled in the high-noon light as they pulled at her boots and mittens. She sat up. There were no parent foxes.

"Fox pups out of the den," she said out loud. "June is old. The baby is due the fifth of July—and I want to be there."

She shouldered her pack and strode off. The fox pups followed her until a ptarmigan flew up; then they turned and pursued it on their long swift legs.

A wolf howled. The voice came from in front of, not behind her. Alarmed, she stopped. Kapu was with her. He had gone ahead to scout the way. He must not do that. She dropped to all fours prepared to meet him eye to eye and forcibly send him back with a stare. Another howl. Julie got to her feet and she burst into laughter.

"Kapugen," she shouted, and broke into a run. "I'm here. I'm here." In the misty distance she could see the stubby outline of her father. He had CB on a leash and was leaning backward as he strained to hold in the dog.

They met with such happiness that CB felt the glee too. He greeted Julie first, jumping up and licking her cheek. She hugged him, then ran into Kapugen's arms.

"The oxen are safe," she said. "The wolves have moose to harvest."

"Moose; they found moose," he said with deep satisfaction. "That is good news, all right," He hugged her again. "Now I have good news for you." Julie waited.

"You have a brother." Kapugen's eyes were shining tenderly.

"A brother," Julie said. "That is good news, all right. What did you name him?"

"Amaroq."

Julie could not speak. She put her fingers to her lips and looked into her father's eyes.

"It is not strange," Kapugen said, seeing her bewilderment. "It is customary among the Eskimos to give the name of a deceased spirit to a baby. Then the baby becomes that one." She frowned, and he went on. "By giving my son the name of your great wolf leader, Amaroq, I have said that he will be like him. Little Amaroq will hunt for himself, he will hunt for his family, and he will defend his tribe against enemies. Like the wolf he will be integrated into the universe."

Julie knew well the Eskimo custom of atiQs, or

namesakes. Babies were often given the names of deceased people. Aunt Martha had been named for a friend who had died, and the friend's family had thought of Aunt Martha as that woman. "You are my grandmother," the family would say to the baby, and no one thought it odd. The spirit of the deceased Martha was present. She was the baby.

"Do you find it strange?" Kapugen asked after Julie had been quiet for many minutes.

"I understand naming a baby after a loved person or a splendid caribou, or strong polar bear," she answered. "But you named your baby after a wolf you did not like and killed. I do not understand that."

"I admired Amaroq," he said. "He died to save Kangik."

"The Minnesota law?" asked Julie softly.

"The Minnesota law."

Julie stood a long moment trying to reconcile the wolf Amaroq's death by repeating over and over to herself, "That is how it is," the Eskimo words that brought acceptance and peace. Finally she looked up at Kapugen.

"The baby will be outstanding," she said. "And"—she looked out across the tundra—"the baby will be my adopted father." She saw once more the magnificent black wolf. His head was lifted, and intelligence lit his eyes. He had just felled a caribou by her camp.

She smiled and thought of his namesake.

"Is the baby's hair red?" she asked curiously.

"Black as the wind cloud."

"And his eyes?"

"Blacker than the new moon."

"He is Amaroq, then," said Julie. "That is good."

"His skin is pale and rosy," Kapugen said. "I hope it does not crack and blister in the sun and cold."

"Ernest Adams's doesn't," Julie said. "His grandfather was a white whaler who came to the Arctic. He is pale, but he does not crack and blister."

Kapugen laughed.

"You are right, all right," he said, shaking his head. "I should not repeat those prejudices. Many Eskimos have white ancestors, and they do not crack and blister any more than the rest of us." He chuckled and leaned down to gather dry grass.

Kapugen cleared a small area on the ground and piled up the grass. Over it he built a tepee of dry sticks he had gathered from streamsides along the way; the kindling had washed down from the mountains, where stunted trees grew. He struck a match to the grass and a flame burst up, licked the driftwood, and set it afire. He opened a large can of store-bought stew, and when the coals were red, he placed it upon them.

"Does Ellen feel well?" Julie asked belatedly.

"She is very well and happy," Kapugen said.

"When was Amaroq born?" she asked.

"June the fifteenth," Kapugen said. "He was a bit early. He caught us by surprise, like the good hunter he is."

"Did you fly Ellen to the hospital?" Julie asked, now eager to learn all the details about the birth of her adopted father.

Kapugen shook his head. "The little wolf decided to be born the day the summer fog rolled in. I could not fly."

"What did you do?"

"I ran for Uma. She came over."

"Uma knows lots about babies," Julie said.

"She does, all right," Kapugen replied, stirring the stew with his hunting knife. "And she knows Eskimo wisdom. She rubbed Ellen's stomach with wolf fur. She said it would give Ellen the power of the female wolf. That is super power," he said, and smiled. "It makes the birth easy and her love for the baby strong."

"Is that what happened?" Julie asked hopefully.

"That is what happened. Six hours later the baby

was born and Ellen was holding him to her breast with fierce love."

"She would do that, all right," Julie said. She could picture Ellen and the little boy with hair as dark as the wind cloud.

"It was then I knew the child was Amaroq. He will be a fine person."

Julie put down her caribou skin and stretched out on her stomach. She watched the fire and thought about little Amaroq. His name bound them all together: herself, the baby, Ellen, Kapugen, the oxen, and the wolves she had led away. They were now one household.

"Aapa," Julie said slowly and cautiously, "what if the wolves come back and kill another musk ox? Now that we have Amaroq with us, will you still go by the Minnesota law? Will you kill them?"

"I must do that," he said.

"Even though we have the little wolf in our house? You would be killing his spirit brothers."

"Industry is under another law," he said. "We must protect it as the wolf protects the game, the plants, and his family."

"That is mixed up," Julie said, and frowned.

"That is how it is in our modern world," said Kapugen.

"Ah, Aapa," she said, looking back toward the mountains. "I hope the caribou return soon."

When the stew was eaten, Julie and Kapugen lay down on their sleeping skins and pulled their parka hoods over their eyes to make their own night. The sounds of July piped across the tundra, as baby birds sang bits of their parents' songs and ground squirrels scurried after berries.

Julie closed her eyes, but she did not sleep right away. She was thinking about baby Amaroq—and Peter.

She was awakened a few hours later by the whacking throb of a helicopter engine. She sat up. The air shook. The whirling wind from the airship's blades twisted her hair and stung her face with dust. She got to all fours and watched as the aircraft, its motor blattering and roaring, started to land not fifty feet away.

Kapugen was up and waving his hands to tell the pilot he and his daughter were present. The pilot saw him, nodded, lifted the craft and set it down two hundred yards away. Kapugen and Julie watched two men climb out of the cabin and walk toward them.

"Morning," the taller of the two said.

"Morning."

"I'm sure surprised to find you here. Sorry about

disturbing you." The man took off his helmet and dark glasses, and Julie saw he was a white man.

"I'm a biologist," he said. "The name's David Bradford. This is my pilot and assistant, Mark. I'm studying the moose. I put radio collars on them so I can track them and learn their numbers and distribution."

Kapugen nodded.

"There's a moose with a collar right around here," he said. "I'm getting a beep on my receiver." He chuckled. "But you two are hardly a moose."

"I am hardly a moose all right," said Kapugen, his eyes twinkling, "and my daughter, Julie, is not a moose either. Don't you know a moose when you see one?" Kapugen laughed out loud. "What a good joke. The biologist finds two Eskimos and thinks they are moose."

"I must admit I did," said David, laughing too. "We heard the beep and followed it. When it was very loud, I looked down and saw a big lump of fur. 'Moose,' I said to Mark.

"When you are eager to see a moose, you see one," he went on, and laughed again. "By any chance have you seen a radio collar? Sometimes they fall off and lie on the ground."

Julie went to her pack. "Are you looking for this?"

she asked, holding up the collar.

"By golly," David said, "this is great. Where did you find it?"

"I found it on a caribou calf," she said. "At least I thought it was a caribou. The animal was so long dead and battered, I could only guess." She looked at him mischievously. "When you are eager to see a caribou, you see a caribou."

David smiled and took the collar. "I put this on a calf only a month ago," he said. "I wonder how the little guy died? Wolves, I would guess."

"Where were you when you put it on him?" Julie asked.

"Along the Colville about twenty miles southwest of here in the river bottomland."

"Then he must have been killed by a grizzly."

"Wolves," David said authoritatively. "I've seen a pack in that area."

"Not the wolves," Julie said. "There is only one pack from Wainwright to the Colville, and I know them well. They would not have gone into the river bottomland. Taboo."

"I'm sure you know a lot about wolves, Julie," David said, smiling condescendingly.

"Julie does know wolves," interjected Kapugen, "like you will never know them. Believe her."

Still David smiled smugly.

"Dave," said Mark, "this man is Kapugen. He is a remarkable hunter and businessman. You can believe him and his daughter. It is said she was lost on the tundra and lived with the wolves and survived."

"Is that true?" David asked with more respect.

"It is true," said Kapugen.

Still skeptical, David took out his notebook, found the date he had tranquilized and collared the calf, and wrote down the date found. After taking a compass reading, he recorded their present location and took Julie's name. He did not fill in the last heading—HOW DIED.

"Do you think you could show me on this topographical map just where you found the radio?" he asked Julie.

"I could do that," she said. Kapugen had such a map on the wall in his bedroom.

"We are here," David said, pointing. "And this is where I collared the calf." He pointed to a spot on the Colville River. Hills rose on each side of it—the mountain beyond was extremely high. It was the area where Julie had led her wolves. Now to find the whelping den on the map. She followed the drainage lines with her finger.

"Here," she said, pointing. "The calf was about

thirty miles from the Colville."

"Grizzly," said David changing his mind. "Wolves carry food to their pups in their stomachs. They don't bring it to them."

"Do grizzlies carry food to their cubs?" asked Kapugen.

"To be honest," David said with some embarrassment, "I don't know. They probably don't. Wolf kill."

"It was not a wolf kill," Julie said. "I see by your notes that the day you put the radio collar on the moose calf, the wolves were in Kangik."

"How do you know such a thing?" David snapped.

"They killed a musk ox," answered Kapugen.

"And," Julie continued, "the wolves were far from the Colville when the calf was killed. A pup was born on the Avalik about that time."

"Why would a bear drag a carcass that far?" David mused.

"She probably didn't," Julie answered. "After killing it, she most likely dragged it inland to her cubs. They feasted and left it, intending to come back. A tender carcass is a treasure to many animals. A fox might have dragged it, an eagle carried it, but I would guess that the wolves found it and brought it back to their pup for a toy. They carry toys in their mouths. Forty miles is a jaunt for a wolf."

"And how did you find it?"

"With my nose," she answered with a grin, knowing she had told only part of the truth.

David wrote down "Death by grizzly" without any more questioning and thanked Julie. He was very pleased with the information she had given him.

"How about our flying you two home?" he asked.

Julie was tempted. She had never ridden in a helicopter.

"Can we, Aapa?" she asked.

"Do you have room for the dog?"

"If you hold him in your lap," Mark answered.

"I will do that, all right," Kapugen said.

David and Mark started toward the copter.

"Speaking of bears," said Kapugen, "there is your lady." He gestured.

Aklaq, the bear, and her two large cubs were on the other side of the helicopter. Mark slipped his rifle out of its scabbard.

The grizzly stood up on her hind legs. Her red tongue emphasized the whiteness of her huge teeth. David jumped into the helicopter. Mark turned to Julie.

"Get in," he said. "I'll scare her away."

The grizzly growled. Then she lowered herself to

the ground and ran straight toward the helicopter. CB barked and snarled. Kapugen picked him up and tossed him into the cabin. Mark went under the copter blades and shouldered his rifle.

Julie threw out her arms, signaling "human."

The rifle boomed.

Another shot followed. The bear roared and bluff charged, then again rose to her hind feet. Before Mark could get off a third shot, Julie was waving her arms at Aklaq and shouting. She walked toward the bear, head down, threatening the big grizzly. Surprised at her aggression, Aklaq dropped to all fours. Her eyesight was poor, but her nostrils were long-range sensors. She smelled gunpowder and Julie's message. Her deepest instincts took hold. She loped back to her cubs, then turned and stood up. She was ready to attack again.

Julie charged her. Aklaq lowered her big feet with the long gleaming claws and walked calmly away as if nothing had happened. Her cubs romped behind her.

"Good girl," Julie said, and walked backward to the helicopter so as not to inspire the bear to chase. She picked up her pack and climbed into the cabin beside Kapugen. CB licked her face.

"How did you know to do that?" Kapugen

proudly asked her. "I did not know you knew how to fend off a bear."

"The wolves taught me," she said. He nodded knowingly, his eyes crackling with pleasure.

The copter motor roared, the blades thrummed, and Julie was lifted up over the tundra.

As the helicopter clattered into the sky, Julie saw Aklaq and her cubs loping southward toward the Colville. A raven scout soared above them on the chance that the bears would scare up a lemming or catch some fish.

Kapugen, in a voice loud enough to be heard over the whack of the helicopter blades, asked David if he would mind flying down the Colville before going home. He wanted to see if there were any solitary caribou in the foothills that he and Malek might harvest. David nodded and told Mark to change course. He needed information on the caribou too.

The noisy machine tipped, hung still in the air like a tern, then sped toward the Brooks Mountains. Looking down, Julie could see the miles of mountain peaks. They were white and jagged like salmon teeth. How wonderful, she thought, to be an animal that could survive in such harsh beauty.

Mark swept the machine low as he followed tree

line on the mountains. After many miles without sighting even one caribou, Kapugen signaled Mark to go to Kangik, and he swung the craft north. David turned around to Kapugen in the rear seat.

"The caribou are over east beyond Prudhoe Bay," he yelled. "A few are starting south, but not toward Kangik."

"They must," Julie whispered to herself. "They must come to Kangik this fall."

"Worrisome spirits," Kapugen said to David. Turning to Julie, he said, "Let's go see the baby." She crinkled her eyes happily.

The helicopter clattered down onto the steel-mesh runway in front of the Quonset. David, who was now much impressed by Julie—particularly because of how she had handled herself with the bear—shook her hand and told her to come to Fairbanks with Kapugen someday. He would show her the radio receivers and the charts he had made for each moose he had collared. He would tell her a lot about moose habits. Then he added, "Or maybe you can tell me." Smiling, he waved good-bye and closed the copter door.

Impatiently Julie waved and waited until the metal insect had lifted off the ground and droned away; then she ran home. Kapugen strode along trying to keep up with her.

"Ellen," she called as she ran into the living room. "Amaroq. Where is he?"

"Sshh—he's sleeping," Ellen said, tiptoeing to a caribou-skin cradle hanging from the ceiling. The little boy's nose and forehead were all Julie could see beneath a soft white fox blanket.

"Amaroq," Julie whispered. "Amaroq." His smooth skin was more pink than white, but his hair was definitely black, very black. His dark eyelashes curled against his fat, round cheeks.

Julie stood quietly before him for a moment, then softly sang,

> "You are my adopted father.
> My feet dance because of you.
> My eyes see because of you.
> My mind thinks because of you.
> And it thinks with your birth
> The wolf and the Eskimo are one again."

Julie looked at little Amaroq a long time. Then she turned to Ellen.

"May I pick him up?"

"No, no," Ellen warned. "Never awaken a sleeping baby, my mother always said."

Julie did not see Kapugen until he was at her side. "Amaroq, Amaroq," he sang as he reached into the cradle and picked up the little boy.

"No, no, Kapugen," Ellen scolded. "Please, let him sleep. He'll be off his routine."

Kapugen rocked the baby in his arms, kissed his soft cheek, and handed him to Julie. She pressed him lovingly to her.

"Dear Ellen," Kapugen said, putting his arm around her shoulder, "there is no routine for babies and children except love and more love."

"Oh, Kapugen," said Ellen. "Our child must be disciplined or he will be like Uma's wild thing."

"Much wilder," said Julie, kissing the baby. "He is Amaroq, the wolf pup. He will pounce and wrestle, even bite. He will run where he pleases as fast as the wind." The baby opened his eyes. They were oval eyes blacker than the new moon and inquiring. He looked right at Julie as if he knew he was her adopted father.

Ellen reached out to rescue her baby. Seeing that she was upset, Julie put Amaroq in his cradle and swung him gently back to sleep.

"Ellen," Julie said softly, never taking her eyes off the baby, "little Amaroq will pounce and snarl and wrestle. He will romp out on the tundra like a caribou calf. You will think he is naughty, but he will be good. All you have to do is call like a mother wolf, and he will come right back. I have seen this."

"I have seen this, too, all right," Kapugen said, checking the thongs on the cradle he had made so that the baby could hang in the midst of the living activities.

Ellen looked at her child and then at Julie.

"Julie," she said, "I have the feeling you believe the spirit of your wolf is in my son."

"He is," Julie said unabashedly. "This is Amaroq." She patted his tiny head.

"Can't you feel his strength?" Kapugen said, taking Ellen's hand and holding it against the baby. "He is strong. He will submerge his personal needs for the good of the whole. That is what the wolf does. The wolf is the only animal that understands the universe. People do not understand it, only amaroq."

"At first," Ellen said, "I did not think you really believed Amaroq's spirit was in our baby." She pulled away from her husband. "Now I see that you do."

"It is so," said Kapugen.

He sat down on the caribou skins and gently drew Ellen beside him. Julie crossed her feet and gracefully sat down, too.

"Close your eyes, Aaka," Julie said. "Kapugen and I have a story to tell you." Ellen clung to Kapugen's hand and closed her eyes.

"See the polar ice cap?" Kapugen said, speaking slowly. "See the earth swell out around the top of the world?" Ellen nodded.

"You are above the North Pole looking down," Julie said slowly. "It is one country up here. Alaska, Canada, Siberia, Greenland, Lappland, all are the same. See it?"

"Yes," Ellen said. "It looks like one country when you look down on the globe instead of up as our maps show it."

"See the ice and wind and animals?" Julie asked. Ellen nodded, eyes still closed.

"Once," Kapugen went on, "two wolves ran and romped. There were no people at that time and no light. The earth was upside down in darkness. One day a raven came to the wolves and told them to hold tight. The raven flew, and as he flew he turned the earth over into the light. The wolves became Eskimos. That is why we are so much like them. We hunt in groups like the wolves. We have leaders like the wolves, and we love our children like they love their pups.

"Since that is so," Kapugen went on, sensing Ellen still could not fathom their words, "it is easy for the wolf to send his spirit into a baby when we give it his name. Child and the wolf spirit live happily."

"Amaroq is here," Julie said, patting the baby. She took the totem from her pocket and held it up for Ellen to see. "Look, he is gone from the totem." Ellen looked, then sighed, trying hard to understand.

"Now, dear Ellen," said Kapugen slowly and carefully, "be a wolf for a moment." She frowned as she tried. "Now, open your eyes. See, Amaroq is that little boy, all right."

Ellen's gray-blue eyes blinked, then widened. She looked from Julie to Kapugen's and then at her sleeping baby.

"I love you both so much," she said helplessly. "But some things are not meant for my understanding. You see what I cannot." Dewlike perspiration arose on her forehead and trickled down the curl by her ear. "I must try to be more like an Eskimo."

"No," Kapugen corrected her. "We must be more like you. To survive in our polar world today, we must join your businesses and learn your language."

Julie looked warily at her father. "Does that also mean we must also go by the Minnesota law?" she asked, her voice low and fearful.

"That too," said Kapugen, and Julie understood that for the good of the village he had adopted the Minnesota law and his heart had frozen solidly around it. She was distressed. When her wolves came

back—and they would; this was their territory—
Kapugen would shoot them. He was telling her that.

Little Amaroq awoke with a cry and the household went into motion. Kapugen held him while
Ellen heated water for his bath and showed Julie how
to lay out his paper diapers.

Peter came in the door. Since no one had heard
his knock, he had taken it upon himself to enter. He
stood quietly for quite a while.

"Julie," he finally said, stepping over to her and
whispering into her ear. "Are the wolves safe? Did
you lead them to game?" She turned in surprise, then
laughed at herself for being so involved with the
baby.

"Ee-lie, I did." she said, happy to see him. "Come
here and meet Amaroq Kapugen. He has only an Eskimo name."

Shyly, Peter crossed the room and looked down at
the little baby kicking and screaming on the table.

"He's a very small wolf leader," he said, and Julie
and Kapugen laughed with great enjoyment.

"I give up," said Ellen. "He *must* be Amaroq. You
say so too, Peter?"

"Of course," said Peter.

Peter picked up a silver rattle Ellen's mother had
sent from Minnesota and shook it, beating out an

Eskimo drummer's rhythm. Kapugen began to sing, Julie hummed, and the baby gurgled softly as he listened to the sounds of the world into which he had been born.

When little Amaroq was washed, dressed, and nursing, Peter took Julie's hand and danced her into the qanitchaq. He closed the door and kissed her on her lips. Her heart raced and her cheeks grew warm. She stepped back. So this is what Ellen had meant when she had said she and Kapugen had fallen in love. She had not understood until now.

"Julie," Peter said in a low voice, "now that the wolves are far away, I can go on with my plans."

"What are they?" Julie asked.

"I am going to school in Fairbanks. I have been admitted to the University of Alaska." Julie felt a pang of disappointment, which Peter quickly saw in her eyes.

"It will be all right," he said, holding her face in his hands. "We'll be together. Ellen sent in your application to the high school in Fairbanks. She said you would be accepted."

"But I can't go," she said, coming to her senses.

"You must," he said.

"The caribou are far away at the Canadian border, Peter."

"What does that mean?"

"That they will not be coming to Kangik. The wolves will come back, and when they do, Kapugen will shoot them."

"It cannot be helped," Peter said. "You must go to school. You want to go to school. I can feel it."

"Yes," she answered. "I do." She opened the outer qanitchaq door and they strolled out into the sunshine. "I want to study to be a teacher and teach Yupik and Iñupiat to the Eskimo children so they will not lose their identity. They are forgetting the language, you know."

"Then you must come with me."

"Who will tend the musk oxen with Malek when you and I are gone?" she asked. "Kapugen is too busy."

"Malek has asked a young nephew to come to Kangik," said Peter.

"I must stay here," she said. Peter pondered as they walked toward the treeless riverbank.

"You could go to school in Barrow, Miyax," he said. "That is not far away by air. You could come home weekends and tend the oxen."

"Barrow?" Julie sat down abruptly on Kapugen's boat.

"What is the matter?" he asked, sitting beside

her. "You seem frightened. Please tell me."

Julie took a breath. "I once lived in Barrow. I was married," she said. "We were married according to the old Eskimo custom, an agreement between parents." She looked at him. "I was not happy. We were never partners."

Peter took her hand. "In Provideniya you would not be married. Two people must agree to make a marriage."

"We did not," Julie said forcefully. "That is why I went out on the tundra. We were too young and I was not ready to marry. I left Barrow to walk to Point Hope and take a boat to San Francisco.

"I would feel uncomfortable in Barrow," she said.

"A good reason to go to in school in Fairbanks," Peter said enthusiastically.

"Not yet."

"Is it because of the wolves?" Peter asked.

"That is a lot of the reason," she said. "But I can learn a lot from Ellen. She has lots of books and music." Both were silent for a long time.

"Come to Fairbanks, Miyax," Peter pleaded softly.

Julie got to her feet and smiled. "Peter," she said in a clear voice, "tell Malek I will take care of the musk oxen while you are gone."

"We are in love," he said, rising and pulling her gently to her feet. He put his arms around her, and she rested her head on his chest.

"I must stay in Kangik," she answered. Peter kissed her warmly, then lifted her chin until he was looking into her eyes. She looked back at him without blinking.

"You are right," he said, dropping his hands to his side. "I can see that you cannot go to school this year. I will miss you." He looked away as if seeing his future a little differently now. "I'll study hard; then I'll come back and marry you and we'll make our own industry. We are good cooperators."

Julie smiled and looked at the river. It ran black through the land.

"When do you leave, Peter?"

"I go next week. Kapugen is taking me. I will find a place to live and work until the end of August, when school begins. I will improve my English." He took her hands. She felt the pressure of his warm fingers; then a bright light shone in his eyes.

"We still have time to get married, lovely Miyax," he said.

"It is a strange thing, Peter," she said thoughtfully. "I find I have acquired a bit of white culture. I get angry with Kapugen for adopting the Minnesota law of the white men, but I find their custom of being older before marriage is a very good thing. That is a good plan the white families have."

Arms around each other, they walked to the river and watched the ciscos streak swiftly past in waves like northern lights. Peter scratched his head.

"Miyax," he said, "I still think you should come to school with me. Kapugen will not shoot Kapu, now that he is related to him through his own son, Amaroq. That would be a difficult thing for him to do."

"But he will," said Julie. "Because he believes the white men are right about wolves and the prey."

"That I do not understand," said Peter. "Kapugen knows we must live with nature, not control it."

Julie looked at this tall young man with the high cheekbones and bronze skin and knew she loved him very much. She also knew he would come back for her when she was ready.

Peter left Kangik. He kissed Julie good-bye, holding her so close she wondered if the old Eskimo ways weren't the best after all. It would be many years before she finished high school and college. The ways of the white people, she mused with a sigh, were not the ways of nature.

But nature still dominated in Kangik. The musk oxen had to be fed, and Ellen needed help with baby Amaroq. And the wolves—the wolves were still somewhere out there in the wind and grass, and if the caribou did not return in the October migration, they were a threat to the musk oxen and thereby themselves.

Almost every evening Julie walked far up the river and howled her I'm-Julie call. Then she waited, holding her breath and listening. When the pack did not answer, she breathed again. They had not come back that night.

In early September snow fell and stayed on the ground. It was the month when the caribou lose the velvet on their antlers. The river iced over and the freeze-up was upon the Arctic.

On a clear afternoon a voice on the CB reported "lots of aiviq in a cove north of Icy Cape." This was good news for Kangik. Walrus was not a favorite food, but it was nourishing and, fortunately for the villagers, not too far away.

Walrus ride the ice floes of the Arctic Ocean that circle endlessly clockwise around the Polar ice cap. When Kapugen heard of their arrival at Icy Cape, they were on their way from their summer feeding grounds in the Arctic Ocean to their overwintering waters in the Bering Sea. There they would dive for clams and loll along the coastal shores until the breakup circled them north again.

"Atik, good afternoon, Atik. Do you hear me?" Kapugen spoke into the CB. "Let us go get aiviq for Kangik."

"I hear you, Kapugen. That is a good plan, all right."

Kapugen harnessed the dogs to a sled loaded with hunting and camping gear, then hooked onto it the sled carrying his sealskin boat. Elated to be going on the last hunt of the year, he went inside to find Julie.

"Miyax," he said, "would you come with us? We could use your help with the camp and the dogs." She slid off the iglek, happy to be asked. Then she hesitated.

"Who will help Ellen?" she asked.

"Uma is coming over," Kapugen said. "She will also check the musk oxen while we are gone." Julie still hung back.

"Ee-lie, little Miyax," he said, his eyes bright. "I spoke to David Bradford. He said he saw the Kangik wolves yesterday."

"Where were they?"

"Down in the bottomland feasting on a moose kill." He smiled. "You made them happy wolves."

Hearing that, Julie quickly dressed in her warmest clothing, truly delighted to be going to the sea ice, the spiritual home of the Yupik Eskimos.

Little Amaroq fussed and she picked him up, patted his straight, sturdy back, and hummed to him. Ellen hurried out of the bedroom.

"Let him cry, please, dear," she said. "He must learn routine and discipline." Julie respected Ellen's wishes. She kissed him and put him back in his cradle, then hurried into the qanitchak to put on her boots. She could not bear to hear the little boy cry.

In the low light of late afternoon Julie, Kapugen, and Atik set out across the frozen tundra. They stopped that night at a well-used campsite of the Eskimo hunters. The next afternoon they arrived at the cove.

Julie helped Atik set up the sleeping tent while Kapugen crept on his belly to a mound above the beach. He wiggled back to say he had counted nine walruses on a floe close to shore.

"How many shall we take?" Atik asked him.

"Two," Kapugen replied. "That is all we need."

"But the ivory," Atik said. "Two sets of tusks will bring fourteen hundred dollars for the corporation. Six will bring forty-two hundred dollars."

"Two," said Kapugen, lifting his head high like a

wolf leader. Atik understood the matter was settled and said no more.

"Miyax," Kapugen said, turning to Julie, "I need your help, all right. There is a female walrus on the floe with a calf that's in trouble. It has fallen into a crevasse. When we shoot, the herd will dive into the sea and the calf will be stranded. We'll be too busy to rescue it. You must try."

"I will try," she said. "I do not know walrus talk, but they must know Yupik. They have been hearing it on all sides of the Arctic Ocean for ten thousand years." Kapugen smiled at her.

"Walruses go *mooo*," said Atik, and winked.

"Let us go," said Kapugen, getting down on his belly to keep out of sight of the walruses. Julie and Atik followed his lead. The light would linger for several more hours, although the sun had set. The afterglow at this time of year brightened the land until almost nine o'clock. The temperature was five above zero. They slithered up the embankment soundlessly.

Suddenly there was a loud hammering sound. Julie lifted her head. Kapugen pushed up on his hands. The dogs barked soft *woofs* to say they were not certain what was abroad in the twilight. There was a pained bellow.

"That's a cry of desperation, " Kapugen said, and

the three, using their elbows and toes to push, wiggled noiselessly up the shore mound. At the top they looked out on a thinly iced sea and nine adult walruses on a floe near shore. Eight were males; the other was the huge mother walrus, her neck and shoulders wreathed in rolls of fat. She was bellowing and cracking the ice floe. Her canine teeth, two enormous gleaming white tusks, were her axes. Chips as big as snow geese were flying in the air as she sought to rescue her calf from the crevasse. Her flexible hind flippers braced her as she worked. She was demolishing the ice before their eyes.

Near her lolled two huge bulls.

Kapugen looked at Atik. Atik looked at Kapugen. Kapugen's eyes said, "Shoot," and they did. It was all over quickly. Two bulls were dead. As Kapugen had predicted, the rest of the herd plunged off the floe and crashed through the slushy ice into a wave of purple water. All but the mother. She did not leave. Paying absolutely no attention to the shots or her dead companions, she kept splintering the ice to free her baby.

She worked on as Kapugen and Atik ran down to the water's edge with the skin boat. Nor did she stop her frantic efforts when Julie stepped into the boat with the hunters and paddled.

Kapugen leaped to the floe and roped his bull. Atik secured his bull. Julie crept forward to try to lasso the calf and pull it out of the cravasse. With that, the female became concerned. She roared at Julie and Kapugen, opening and closing her mouth rapidly and making the jackhammer sound again. Then she bluff charged.

Kapugen and Julie stood still. The walrus glared at them out of her mournful eyes, turned away, and frantically slashed the far side of the crevasse. In less time than it took Julie to wind her rope to toss, the great tusks had demolished the sea side of the ice floe. The calf was free. It slipped into the water. The mother plunged in after it, lifted it up on her back, and swam off.

"So much for my job," said Julie, watching the mother and calf. "She didn't need any help at all." She smiled in admiration.

Kapugen rested his hand on Julie's shoulder. She looked up and saw that his eyes were shadowy with dreams as he watched the fearless mother walrus swim away. Even after she had disappeared among the floes, Kapugen still did not take his eyes from the icy spot where she had vanished. Finally he spoke.

"Once the elders told me this," he said very slowly. "We are all related." He gestured toward the

caring mother. "They were right, all right."

"Yes," said Julie. "They were right, all right."

Something had happened to Kapugen, Julie realized. Here on the bleak and lonely shore the mother walrus had brought him back from the white man's land. She slipped her hand into his, and her shivering fingers warmed.

Suddenly they were in great danger. One half of the floe was gone, and the half on which they stood was tipping. The tethered bulls slid toward the sea. Kapugen eased one into the water with the rope, trying to stabilize the floe, but it was too late. It began to roll over. Atik leaped into the boat and pulled his walrus into the sea. Kapugen picked up Julie, threw her into the boat, and jumped in after her.

They paddled landward slowly, hindered by the one-ton walruses. Behind them the floe kept tipping until it was straight up like a breaching whale. Then it fell. Julie saw it was about to crash onto Atik's walrus and pull boat and hunters down into the sea. With a swift movement she severed the rope with her ulu. The floe thundered down upon the bull, and he disappeared from sight. Kapugen shot Julie a grateful glance.

They beached the boat. Kapugen and Atik jumped ashore and hauled the remaining walrus to safety. For a moment the three hunters stood quietly looking at the huge animal, each thinking his own thoughts.

After a respectful silence Kapugen took out his man's knife and slit open the belly. He reached into the warm body, found the heart, and carried it to the sea edge.

"Great Aiviq," he said. "I have borrowed your body. My flesh will be your flesh." He threw the heart into the waves. "I return your spirit to the sea. I give you birth again."

When the ceremony of respect was done, Kapugen and Atik got into the boat and paddled out to rescue the other walrus. It was a terrible thing to kill an animal and not use it. They paddled around the floe searching the water but could not find the dead walrus.

"I apologize, Aiviq," Kapugen said in his low, slowly paced voice. "I am sorry I wasted you. I shall walk around the house four times when I return to punish myself for losing you." Julie listened and felt peaceful. This was the father she remembered.

"I am very sorry, Aiviq," Atik said. "Your hide was to be a beautiful boat cover, your intestines to be rain gear, your flesh my flesh. I am sorry."

When they were on shore again, Kapugen and

Atik removed the two smooth white tusks, then butchered the huge animal into portions for Kangik.

"You can still make your boat cover," Kapugen said to his friend as they carried the hide to the sled. "This is for you." Atik smiled his thanks. The Eskimo languages have no words for "thank you." One does not give to be thanked. A person gives to please himself; that requires no thanks.

When the skin was on the sled and the meat packed, Atik picked up the intestines and packed them.

"Uma will make little Amaroq a raincoat of these intestines," he said. "She was going to do that if I brought an aiviq home."

In the pitch blackness Atik lit the Coleman stove and placed a large piece of walrus meat in a pot for a harvest dinner. Julie fed the dogs their portion. They ate happily, wagging their tails. The stars shone like huge silver lights as the hunting party feasted and the moon circled around the sky. Kapugen looked up in thoughtful silence.

The next morning the hunters packed their meat, ivory, tent, and gear and faced the dogs toward Kangik.

"Hut," Julie called, and barking and leaping, CB

in the lead, they took off for Kangik full of the energy of the walrus.

The days grew quickly shorter.

"Taggaqtugik," Julie said to Ellen on the first of November. "That means 'the month when the lakes are frozen and you can see your reflection on the ice.'"

"Very pretty," said Ellen, burping Amaroq on her shoulder.

"It is also the month," said Julie, "when all the whales are south in the Bering Sea, when the pregnant polar bears come inland to dig dens in the snow. It is the month when the seals swim under the sea ice and the only birds that remain with us are the snowy owls and the guillemots.

"Except for ice fishing," she said, "the time of food gathering is over."

The sun did not rise on November eighteenth, and everything turned blue—the snow, the footprints, the shadows. The Arctic night was a palette of blues.

Julie, Ellen, and little Amaroq went to school every weekday. Ellen put the baby on a warm polar-bear skin on the table, and lessons began.

With Amaroq to inspire the teacher, the ten children of all ages learned such English sentences as "The baby sees his toes" and "The baby needs diapering." From Julie they learned how to say the same thing in Iñupiat and Yupik. Julie also showed them how to add five baby fingers and five baby fingers to get ten. She followed this with a lesson on how to take away four baby toes from five. Ellen taught them to sing "The Far Northland."

An important lesson was devised by the North Slope Education Department. Each child was given ten dollars. With it they bought stock in the Kangik School Corporation. Then Marie came to the school to set up an Eskimo doughnut business. She paid for the flour and ingredients by writing out a corporation check, financed by the children's investment stock. She and the students mixed and cooked doughnuts. When they were done, the children ran through the village streets, following the lights through the blackness to homes, and sold the doughnuts to Kangik families. With the money they took in, they paid the corporation back for the ingredients. Then each child was paid a five-cent commission. The rest was profit. It went into the corporation. In this way they learned about the native corporations that had been supporting the Alaskan Eskimos and Indians since 1971.

A letter from Peter to the children of Kangik arrived at the school one December day, and Ellen asked Julie to read it aloud.

"Dear friends," the letter began. "I am in Fairbanks in a student room on the campus of the University of Alaska. We eat in a big dining room and go to classes. I am taking four courses—English, biology, mathematics, and sociology. Each one is in a different building.

"Miyax asked me to tell you about my Siberian village. You would feel at home there. It looks very much like Kangik. My father wears maklaks and parkas and hunts for polar bears and walrus. My mother wears traditional clothing and makes our food. In Russia we have to borrow guns from the government when we go hunting. We have to bring back the empty shells when we turn in the guns. For that reason my father uses traps and spears to hunt.

"I miss you all." Before Julie could stop, she read: "Tell Julie that I love her and that I am her forever-partner. Your friend, Peter."

She blushed and picked up little Amaroq to hide her embarrassment.

"Peter loves Julie," said Marie's adopted eight-year-old, Bessie, and the children giggled and broke into a chant. Ellen clapped her hands, and the school day was over. Hastily Julie dressed them in their warm overclothes to much teasing and laughter and sent them all home.

After the last child had zipped up his parka and stepped out into the cold wind and darkness, another school day began. Ellen taught Julie world history and mathematics, and Julie taught Ellen Yupik and Iñupiat.

Julie closed the Iñupiaq-and-English dictionary at the end of their study period and took Peter's letter out of her shirt. Smiling shyly, she looked at it.

"What do you think of Peter, Aaka?" she asked.

"I like him," Ellen said.

"Why does he keep saying he loves me?"

"I think he does."

"He has school to attend, and when the caribou return to Kangik, I have school to attend. We are not ready to make an iglu."

"Do you love him?"

"Not yet," Julie said. "Kapugen will not let me."

"Julie," Ellen said in shock, "why do you say that? You know Kapugen wants you to grow up and love and marry. You know that."

"He does, but he stops me." She put the dictionary on the desk. "I must stay here in Kangik so he doesn't kill the wolves. I cannot think about Peter or school as long as he is thinking about the Minnesota law."

"Oh, Julie," Ellen said, looking down at the gurgling Amaroq. "I am sorry to hear you say that."

Julie looked at her father's wife. This stepmother she loved so much did not know what every Eskimo knew from birth: that people and animals coexist for the welfare of both.

In early April a warm wind from the east brought rain that turned the snow to slush. The villagers took off their heavy parkas and visited in the community yard and along the river. They wondered if the early spring would bring the caribou to Kangik.

Then a blast of below-zero air hit like the sting of a scorpion's tail. Land, slush, and water froze in an hour. An icy rain put down a covering of ice. Kangik, its houses, boats, and sleds were under a sheath of glass. Doors were frozen shut. Walking was treacherous, and food caches were almost impossible to open. This was the worst possible weather in a land of impossible weather conditions.

The freeze dropped below minus thirty degrees and held for almost a month. Kapugen's plane could not fly at that temperature and food became a problem. Marie's store ran out of supplies. Atik, who still had frozen walrus meat on his sled, switched on his CB.

"Atik has walrus meat," he said. "Come to my sled at my house if you want walrus meat. Out." Not long after the announcement, qanitchak doors were kicked open and children with plastic bags and adults with pots skidded and skated to Atik's for a share of his harvest.

One night the electricity went out. Marie had to walk to Kapugen's house to tell him she was out of gasoline for the generator. The villagers lit candles for light and their camp stoves for cooking. They turned their coal-oil heaters low to conserve oil. The weather station reported no change in temperature.

Several of the hungry children became sick. When the temperature rose to minus twenty degrees, Kapugen lit the kerosene heaters in the Quonset and warmed up his airplane. The men from the village helped chip ice off the runway, and he and Malek took off for Barrow to purchase supplies. Ellen's last words, as he left the house, were "Pampers, please, bring Pampers."

In Barrow, Kapugen rented a Beaver, the workhorse plane of the north, and loaded it with gasoline, heating oil, alfalfa pellets for the musk oxen, and boxes of groceries. He paid for them with a corporation check. At the U.S. weather station in Barrow he was told that the forecast for the day was clear and would hold at minus twenty degrees.

"A good time for flying," Kapugen said. "We can go to the Brooks Range and see if the caribou herd is coming north."

With a catlike purr the big Beaver took off, and Kapugen headed it south to the Colville. He saw no caribou in the foothills or along the river.

On the way back to Kangik Kapugen spotted a gang of ravens and a lonesome wolverine. That was all. No moose, no caribou. Disappointed, he flew home, landing safely on the still-icy Kangik airstrip.

Kapugen and Malek were planning to call for help in unloading supplies, but did not have to. Everyone had heard the Beaver arrive, and men and women were streaming across the tundra, pulling their sleds, ready to help.

Kapugen did not go to his house until the generator was going again and the supplies were in the store. He then joined Ellen and Julie. Unable to tell them that the caribou would not come again this year, he picked up sleeping Amaroq and held him in his arms. The baby opened his eyes.

"I have a song for you," Kapugen said to his little son. "Listen to me.

"O caribou, where are you hiding?
I know where you walk.
In the darkness of the trees,
In the passes, in the tundra grass,
I know where you walk."

He held the baby against his shoulder and patted his firm body.

"O caribou, where are you hiding?
I cannot wait—my children are hungry.
I know where you walk.
In the darkness of the trees,
In the passes, in the tundra grass,
I know where you walk.
You will not come to Kangik,
Aya, ya, ya, you will not come to Kangik."

"Aya, ya, ya," sang Julie, in sadness and fear for the village's well-being. "You will not come to Kangik."

"Aya, ya, ya," sang a voice from the qanitchak. Kapugen handed little Amaroq to Julie and opened the inner door.

"David Bradford," he said to the Fish and Game man. "Do you bring us good news? Are the caribou coming to Kangik?"

"I've come to see how you all are faring in this

treacherous weather," he said, not answering the question. "But I can see you are okay."

"Come in," called Ellen. "I'll make tea. You must be cold."

Julie nodded to him and smiled.

"Hello, little bear lady," he said to her. Ignoring his greeting, she held up the red-cheeked Amaroq for him to admire.

"So this is your little brother, Julie," David said. "He looks as strong as a wolf's jaw."

"And he is," said Julie, laughing at the idea of a baby being compared to a wolf's jaw.

David sat down in the overstuffed chair and gratefully accepted a steaming cup of tea from Ellen. He warmed his hands on it.

"Terrible weather," he said. "I had to leave the copter running or I'll never get it started again, so I can't stay long.

"What I've come to say, Kapugen, is that those wolves you said killed your musk ox left the Colville and are headed this way."

Julie's heart thumped.

"I thought I'd warn you before they kill another."

"That is good to know," said Kapugen, slowly rising and picking up his gun. "I will intercept them before they get here."

"No, Aapa, no," Julie cried, running to her father. "You promised you would not kill them unless they killed another musk ox. They have not killed one." She hugged little Amaroq closer. "Let me take them away again. You promised."

Kapugen frowned.

"I did say that, all right," he said. "But I am like the wolf. I must defend my family from the enemy."

"The wolves are not our enemy, Aapa," Julie whispered. "You know that. They are part of us. We are part of them." She put her cheek against the soft, smooth head of the baby. He arched back and bawled.

"Even little Amaroq," she said, patting him to calm him down, "knows you should not shoot the wolf."

"Well, that is one interpretation," said Ellen from her seat at the table, where she was correcting school papers. "I would say little Amaroq is crying because his father woke him up."

"Ayaa, I woke him up," said Kapugen, smiling and putting down his gun. He gently took his son from Julie and placed his forehead against the small nose. "You do not mind, do you, little wolf pup?" Amaroq stopped crying and kicked his feet.

Julie scrambled up on the iglek. Her thoughts

were interrupted by the conversation between Kapugen and David. They were planning how best to intercept the wolves and shoot them. Ellen listened too.

"I've got to return the Beaver before I can do anything," said Kapugen.

"You have time," David said. "The pack was feeding on something in a watershed of the Avalik River. They ought to sleep a day or two."

David walked to the door. "I've got to get to Barrow," he said. "I have to examine a polar bear that killed a white man there." Kapugen's face did not show any expression.

"That is how it is," he said softly. "Where was the gussak?"

"Right near his house on the beach. He had gone out to start his car. A polar bear charged him, and he turned and ran. That was a mistake. Julie taught me not to run. He did not make it."

"Did they get the bear?" asked Kapugen.

"His neighbor shot the bear."

"Dangerous time of year," said Kapugen. "The polar bear mothers are rejecting their two-year-old cubs—and they are hungry."

"And so are the wolves," said David before putting on his face mask and dark glasses. He opened the door, and cold air from the qanitchaq ballooned into the room. Ellen shuddered.

"I don't think I'll ever get used to cold," she said, and laughed. "Or is it the forces moving in the wilderness that make me shiver?"

Julie did not speak.

"I'm ready," called Malek from outside. "Time to take the Beaver back." Kapugen turned to Ellen. "Malek and I are going to return the rented plane and bring back mine to Kangik."

"Hurry, before the wolves come," she said. Kapugen nodded his head once. His eyes did not shine. He put little Amaroq in his cradle and kissed his booted foot. Then he left.

When Julie and Ellen were alone, Julie came down from the iglek and sat beside her.

"Ellen," she said, "our next lesson is about how every beast and plant is dependent on every other beast and plant."

"I understand that," she said. "You have taught me well."

Julie despaired. She had been talking to Ellen since the sun had gone down about cycles and the rise of one animal and the fall of another. She had held up her hands and told her how the Eskimo knew they were related to all the animals because they all had the same bones in one shape or another. She had told her that wolves keep the environment healthy, and that when the environment is healthy, people are healthy.

And still Ellen had told her she would kill a wolf to save the oxen and Kapugen agreed with her.

Julie knew she must do something right now. "When things are not working, you are doing something wrong," she had said to herself on the tundra. "Change what you are doing." She looked long at Ellen and took a deep breath.

"Dear Ellen," she said. "I will stop lecturing and tell you a story.

"A young girl was lost on the tundra. She was starving. One day she found the summer nursery of a wolf pack and made friends with the wolves. A puppy taught her how to get food from the wolves' stomach baskets by touching the corner of a wolf's mouth. She did that, and a wolf generously gave up food for her, but the food was not enough. She ate moss and fungi.

"A fog rolled over the land and she could not see. The earth vibrated. The fog thinned and Kapu, her puppy friend, came into view. As alert as an eagle, he was sniffing the wind and wagging his tail as if reading some amusing wolf story. She sniffed, too, but for her the pages were blank." Julie looked into Ellen's eyes.

"Amaroq, the great leader of the wolf pack, howled. Nails, his best friend, bark-howled. Then Amaroq slid into a musical song and Silver, his mate, joined in. Their voices rose and fell as each harmonized with the other. The windy voice of Jello, the baby-sitter, crooned, and like the beat of drums, the five pups whooped and yipped. The girl rubbed her chin; something was different about this hunt song. It was eerie and restless. It spoke of things she did not understand, and she was frightened.

"The fog cleared again and she saw Amaroq, his hunters, and the pups running across the tundra. Even Jello was with them. Were they leaving her? Was this their day to take up the wandering life of the wolves? Was she now on her own? She crawled around her frost heave and frantically gathered the leafy plants that the caribou eat. She stuffed mushroomlike fungi into her pocket, and bits of reindeer moss. She could no longer pass up anything that might be edible.

"As she worked on her hands and knees, the vibrations in the earth grew stronger. The girl drew back. Out of the fog came a huge caribou running her way. At his neck, leaping with the power of an ocean wave, was Amaroq." Ellen glanced around the room. Her eyes fell on the spot where Kapugen had put down his gun. It was gone. Julie went on.

"Nails was diving in and out under the caribou. At his flank was Silver.

"Then Amaroq jumped, floated in the air for an instant, and sank his teeth into the shoulder of the beast.

"The fog closed in briefly, and when it thinned, the caribou was poised above Amaroq, his cleaverlike hoofs aimed at his head. There was a low grunt, a flash of hoofs, and the huge feet cut uselessly into the sod; for Amaroq had jumped again and sunk his teeth into the animal's back. Snarling, using the weight of his body as a tool, he rode the circling and stumbling beast. Silver leaped in front of the bull trying to trip him and slow him down. Nails had a grip on one hind leg. The caribou bucked, writhed, then dropped to his knees. His antlers pierced the ground. He bellowed and fell.

"Miyax, the girl, could not believe her good fortune—an entire caribou felled practically at her feet. This was enough food to last her a month, perhaps a year. She would smoke it to make it lighter to carry, pack it, and walk on to the coast. She would live.

"And I did."

Ellen sat very still. Presently she got up to look for Kapugen's gun in the qanitchaq. It was not there.

"Julie," she said, "I understand. I understand. Please go tell Kapugen I am wrong: The Minnesota law does not work here."

Julie put on her warm qivit pants and sweater. Over these she pulled her down pants and parka. Then she put on her wool cap, gloves, and mittens. She stuffed her pockets with jerky and went out into the glaring ice world. She walked to the sled she had loaded with alfalfa pellets last night, and rather than take the dogs over the treacherous ice, she picked up the rope and pulled the sled herself. She slipped a few times, then got her footing. After she fed the musk oxen, she was going to go out on the tundra to find Kapu and Aaka, Silver, Raw Bones, Zing, and Amy, and turn them away. She glanced at the Quonset and listened for the doors to open and for Kapugen to start up the Beaver. He would be able to shoot well from that plane.

At the corral she dumped the pellets in the feed trough, closed the gate, struggling for a moment with the icy bolt, then headed for the riverbank. She had not gone five paces before she stopped. Kapugen had been here. His boots, with the distinctive crimping on their soles, had broken through the ice layer and left their imprints in the snow. He was here with his gun. He was not taking the Beaver to Barrow. His footsteps were fresh and led off around the corral. He was stalking the wolves on foot.

A howl sounded in the distance. It was followed by an alert bark, and then, urgently, the voices of her wolves rose from the tundra wilderness. She ran toward them. The ice broke under her feet, slowing her down, but she plugged on, determined to save them somehow.

What can I do? How can I scare them? A gun would help. I have none. A dead wolf would work—my wolf-head mittens perhaps. They're at home. She noted that the wind was blowing her scent in the direction of Kapu and his pack. She hoped he would smell her and the fear odor she was exuding. That would turn them away. She struggled, looking back to see if Kapugen was following.

The earth shook, a crackling roar sounded. Julie turned around again, to see the musk oxen thundering out of the corral, bulls first, calves in the middle, cows bringing up the rear. Their skirts flowing in the wind, they rushed out onto the tundra and headed for a knoll above the river. They had escaped. They were free. For a moment Julie was thrilled; then she was frightened.

The industry was gone. Kapugen had failed. Little Amaroq would not have a future. She must drive the herd back to the corral. Running, stumbling, she tried to swing around them with flying arms and shouts. Snow burst up from their feet, obscuring them and the corral. She ran.

A shimmer appeared on the river ice. Julie dropped to all fours and focused as her wolf pack, Kapu in the lead, the others behind, trotted down the frozen river. They moved like flowing water. They left the riverbed and dashed into the ox herd. Weaving among them, pacing their own steps to the steps of the wing-footed bulls, Kapu and his pack sized up the herd.

The cloud of snow the oxen had stirred settled down. Julie rubbed her eyes. Kapugen was standing beside the corral. He had no gun. His hands were clasped behind his back, his head forward.

Julie looked from him to the wolves. They were loping along easily as they scattered the herd. She didn't understand why the oxen hadn't formed a defense ring. They were making themselves easy targets by scattering. She closed her eyes, not wanting to see what came next.

When she opened them, the wolves were walking. The musk oxen had stopped running. They cracked the ice with their huge hoofs and leaned down to browse serenely on the emerging tundra grass. The wolves, panting and wagging their tails, trotted off a short distance and lay down on their bellies.

For some unknown reason the hunt was over. There would be no kill. The predator knew something that was not for Julie's understanding.

Then she saw that the gate was open.

Had she left it ajar? she wondered frantically. Had she not locked it tight enough? No, she remembered the difficulty she had had in throwing the bolt in the cold. She had locked it well.

And then she knew.

Kapugen had set the musk oxen free.

She walked across the ice to him, pulling the sled behind her.

"There they are again," he said. "The wolf and the little oxen of the north."

For a long quiet hour Julie and her father watched the animals moving beneath a white sun that shone down on the top of the earth.

"The industry, Aapa," Julie whispered. "What will happen to the industry?"

"We now have a wild herd," he said. The look on his face was peaceful.

"The Eskimo wiped out the musk oxen of Alaska

when the white men gave us guns. Now the Eskimo has restored them. They will live and reproduce and become part of us again." He turned to her. "As for the industry, you and I will have to walk a lot farther, as our people used to do, to gather the qivit for the knitters. That is all."

He added slowly, "But I don't know what Ellen will say."

"I have just left her," Julie said. "She has said the Minnesota law is not the law of the Arctic. She thinks so, all right."

"Then I think so too, all right," said Kapugen, squinting out over the magnificent tundra, his home.

The wind buffeted them but they did not leave. Like the musk oxen and wolves, they, too, had been restored to order.

"When are you going to school?" Kapugen finally asked.

"When the caribou return," Julie said.

"They will, all right," said Kapugen. "The wolves have been talking." He pushed back his parka hood and cupped his hands behind his ears. "Listen," he said.

Kapu howled. He began on a low note and climbed to the highest pitch of the wind and held it there. Zing, Silver, Aaka, Raw Bones, and Amy joined in. The air quivered, the ice snapped, and the land crackled with life.

"They are saying," Kapugen said, "that the caribou are coming." Julie shaded her eyes and looked at the river and tundra.

A dark-gray mass quivered on the glare ice. It seemed to be a wind cloud moving toward them. Julie squinted. Above the darkness rode antlers, a sea of them.

"Aapa," she cried. "The caribou are here!"

Like the irresistible force of nature that it is, the female caribou herd surged toward them. The males were days behind. The females carried their heads high, these beasts of the icy past who, together with the wolves and musk oxen, had kept the tundra flourishing for an eon. The breath clouds behind them streamed out like white banners heralding their return. The herd was magnificent to see. Kapu howled one penetrating note and held it. The musk oxen snorted and stared at the tide of caribou without expression, and Kapugen and Julie threw their arms around each other.

"That is how it is," Kapugen said.

As Julie watched the life-bringing caribou caravan, she thought about high school, books, girls, boys, and teachers. Then she felt Peter's whistle

against her chest and she thought about him.

If I can think of school and teachers before I think of Peter, she reasoned, *I am not in love.* But images of little ground squirrels popping out of the earth and the vision of Peter dancing at the Nalukataq festival changed her mind.

"I will marry Peter," she said to herself, "when I am all grown up."

Kapugen picked up the sled rope, Julie took hold, and together they walked back to Kangik. They listened to the howl of the wolf mingling with the tatoo of an Eskimo drummer announcing the return of life.

JEAN CRAIGHEAD GEORGE decided to write this sequel after receiving thousands of letters from children all over North America asking what happened to Julie after she left the wolves. Ms. George's frequent visits to Alaska gave her  the additional inspiration to continue Julie's story.

The author of many beloved books for children, Jean George has also written three ecological mysteries: WHO REALLY KILLED COCK ROBIN?, THE MISSING 'GATOR OF GUMBO LIMBO, and THE FIRE BUG CONNECTION, all available in Harper Trophy editions. She lives in Chappaqua, New York.

WENDELL MINOR's picture books include SIERRA, HEARTLAND, and MOJAVE, all by Diane Siebert; THE SEASHORE BOOK, by Charlotte Zolotow; and EVERGLADES, by Jean Craighead George. Mr. Minor lives in Washington, Connecticut, with  his wife, Florence, and their two cats, Willie and Mouse.